Praise for:

from MOTHER, with LOVE

From Mother with Love
ISBN 1-884667-01-5

Published by LEI Publishing
2673 N. E . 37th Drive
Fort Lauderdale, Florida 33308
888-262-8071

Copyright © 1994 by Dale Ledbetter

Library of Congress Card Number: 00-101597

Cover and content design by Dotti Albertine

from MOTHER, with LOVE

reflections on achieving success in selling

Dale Ledbetter

Published by LEI Publishing
2673 N. E . 37th Drive
Fort Lauderdale, Florida 33308
888-262-8071

This book is dedicated
to the memory of my mother.

~ Acknowledgements ~

To Ron Grubbs who succeeded my mother in her sales territory and shared many stories about her with me.

To Roberta Ruggiero without whose help and support this project could not have been completed.

To Myra Mahoney, Linda Nobilski and Sheri Gordon for their commitment to excellence in typing and editing the manuscript.

CONTENTS

⁓ Introduction ⁓

The celebrated author, Arthur Hailey, wrote <u>Strong Medicine</u>, which was published in 1984. The book centered around the exploits of Celia Jordan, a fictional heroine, who began as a pharmaceutical sales representative and rose to head a pharmaceutical company. Arthur Hailey never met my mother. However, in real life, my mother was, to the best of my knowledge, the first female pharmaceutical salesperson in America.

She was truly a person ahead of her time. She entered into a world which had been totally dominated by men in the past and became a rousing success. Throughout her career, and after she stopped actively selling, she was a constant source of inspiration for me. At one point, she took the time to write a series of letters to me in which she shared the secrets of her success.

Unfortunately, the actual letters were lost during the course of a major move across the country.

However, given the many hours I spent studying the original letters and the constant conversations we had on the secrets of achieving success, I remember the essence of what she was trying to teach me, and I have made every effort to reproduce the letters as closely as possible to the originals.

It is with great pride and gratitude to her that I share them with you.

Chapter One

MOTHER'S PLAN

Dear Son,

Congratulations!

Your decision to embark upon a career in sales is exciting news and has stirred the fires of my enthusiasm. I can't think of a more noble calling, and I am confident that you will derive great personal satisfaction as well as achieve immense financial success in your new profession. Whether you stay in sales or move into the management side of business, the best way I can contribute to your success, as you take on new challenges, is to share with you the many lessons I have learned.

~ from Mother, with Love ~

As you know, I had a considerable amount of success as a salesperson. In the beginning, I did things unconsciously without really thinking about them. I was under great financial pressure to succeed and had very little time to think about what methods worked and which ones did not, or what made me a success and what hampered my progress toward becoming a success. However, after the first few years, and given the success I had, I began to have the luxury of thinking about what I was doing. My approach began to take on a more organized pattern, and I made a conscious effort to analyze what worked and what did not work.

Somerset Maugham once wrote that we need to, *"Learn from the experiences of others because our own make us bitter."* It would not be possible or desirable for you to avoid learning many hard lessons on your own. However, maybe I can soften a few blows for you and help you gain more insight into what occurs along the roads you travel by sharing with you lessons which my adventures and experiences have taught me . Starting next week, I am going to send you one letter per week for 10 weeks, describing, in as much detail as I can recall, one of the ten reasons why I have achieved some degree of success. Please read and think about each lesson and let's talk about your impressions. Also, please give me the chance to answer any questions you may have.

I have often said to you that I plan to write a book some day. These letters will be my "book". If you find the ideas valuable, practical, and worth developing in your own life, perhaps you will combine the ideas with your own experiences and someday convert them into a book. By sharing "my little secrets" with you I can achieve a little bit of immortality. If no one else ever reads my lessons, but you find them worthwhile, then I will be amply rewarded. You be the judge of their value for others. I would be delighted to know that someday you found these ideas worthy of being passed on to benefit others.

Many inspirational materials are too lengthy. I have tried to give you enough detail to make my point, but not so much as to become unnecessarily repetitive. The purpose of these letters will be to inspire action. That goal can be better accomplished with fewer words rather than with many.

These letters will be devoted solely to helping you improve your life and advance your career. I will write separate letters to let you know what is going on at home. I do not want to mix the two in case you period-ically want to reread these lessons for inspiration and guidance. I also want them to be in a form that would permit you to share them with others if you so desire. While each lesson will stand on its own, you will derive the greatest benefit if you approach all ten letters as a total package. You will see, as we go along, how each lesson ties in with the others.

~ *from Mother, with Love* ~

I love you more than you can ever know, at least until the time comes when you have children of your own and are able to appreciate the love of a parent.

Congratulations Again!

All my love,
Mother

Chapter Two

SHARE LOVE

*"You can make more friends in two months
by becoming interested in other people than you can in
two years by trying to get other people interested in you."*
— DALE CARNEGIE

Dear Son,

This is the first of the series of letters I promised. And
what a way to start — by talking about love, my
favorite subject. The first lesson is critically important
for you to master if you are to become successful. As a
by product, understanding this lesson and putting it
into practice will also make you a better person and a
happier human being.

~ from Mother, with Love ~

My experiences and observations have taught me that you must learn to share love. But, you cannot stop there. You must learn to share your feelings of love. Loving is not enough if the object of your affection does not know how you feel. You are like a tree falling in a forest with no one to hear the sound. Practice at home with those you care most about. After you have had children of your own, don't hesitate to pick them up in your arms, hold them and tell them how much you love them. Do the same thing with your wife. If you live away from those you love, write regularly and call often. As a mother, I can tell you that the greatest moment in the world is to hear your voice at the other end of a telephone line telling me that you love me.

If you love someone, tell them so, but go beyond that and show them. Look for ways to show those you care about how much you care about them. Find any excuse to demonstrate how you feel. I've heard friends of mine say after a parent has passed away, "If only I could speak to them now, there is so much I would say." But, alas, it is too late. Don't ever fail to speak or act on your feelings. Never leave yourself in a position to regret what you did not say or do to express your feelings. If you feel it, say it! If you want to show it, don't hold back, do it!

Iris Murdoch, an Irish writer, said it well, *"We can only learn to love by loving."* This same approach should be followed in dealing with your clients. Don't just tell them that you care about them personally or care about their success. Find ways to show them continuously that these are not empty words on your part. Anytime you can convince someone that you truly care about them, and demonstrate your feelings on an ongoing basis, you have laid the ground work for establishing a lasting relationship.

I always sent a weekly communication to each of my clients. I, obviously, could not see them all every week, and I may not have had a reason to send them a direct business communication on a weekly basis. But, by spending a few minutes at night during the week, looking for items in magazines or periodicals which I knew would be of interest to them, and sending copies along with a personal note, I could demonstrate that they were in my thoughts. It was impossible for them to conclude that I was not genuinely interested in them personally and in what they were doing. Even those cynics who might think I did it only to get their business would still appreciate the fact that I took the time to communicate with them on a regular basis about things other than my products and services. I can assure you that few of my competitors ever did as much.

Send books or cards on birthdays, and when your clients are having a baby. Send them a card or letter of congratulations when they achieve, or someone in their family achieves, something significant. I made a habit of looking for articles in the newspaper, and whenever I would see one of my clients or a member of their family mentioned, I would get off a quick note letting them know I was sharing their joy and wanting them to know how good I felt for them. As an example, one of my clients had a son playing Little League baseball. They won the city championship and a team picture appeared in the local paper. I knew from previous conversations how proud my client was of his son who played second base and was one of the leading hitters on the team. I sent him a note telling him how proud I knew he must be. Of all the things I ever did, that one act had the greatest impact on my relationship with that client. He never forgot that I cared enough to take a moment to congratulate him on something that was important to him. He didn't consider for a moment that my expression was phony and designed only to get his business. I can assure you that it was never the case. I had come to know him and his family, and I genuinely cared about their feelings and shared the emotional highs of their successes.

The opposite end of the emotional spectrum is equally important. When tragedies occur, always learn to be there. One of the doctors I dealt with for years lost his wife suddenly in an accident. He was distraught and unable to work for over a month. I called his office repeatedly, leaving messages so that he would know I was concerned about him. I also took time to write him a lengthy letter and sent him several books which were helpful in times of tragedy. He knew I genuinely cared and never forgot what he considered to be great kindness at a very critical time in his life. He was one of my top clients from that time forward. Again, he knew that I was going far beyond trying to develop a relationship with him as a client, and that I genuinely cared about his feelings and well being. If I had not taken the time to let him know how I felt and to show him how deep my feelings were by seeking out appropriate gifts, he would have never known how I really felt about him.

It is important to use the same approach in dealing with your fellow employees. I had a sales manager who would come in from the home office to work with me for at least one week every three months. On a semi-annual basis he would also conduct a sales meeting which would bring together all the representatives in our region. Within the first year of my employment, as a result of these meetings, I felt a great sense of closeness with every one of my fellow sales representatives. I sincerely felt that they were an extended family to me. I credit my sales manager with creating this environment. It didn't just happen. He went to extraordinary lengths to create the feeling of "family" which we all felt.

When he came to work with me, he would always arrive on Sunday evening. I would meet him for breakfast on Monday morning to preview the week for him, tell him who we were going to see and what I hoped to accomplish during the week. He would also bring information on new products or approaches and share new ideas from other representatives within the region. However, we never began the breakfast by talking about any of those things. His first question was always "How are you?" This wasn't a perfunctory greeting but a sincere solicitation as to my current health and state of mind. He would expect a thorough answer from me detailing what had taken place in my life since our last meeting. He wanted to know how you were doing in school and would remember to ask about your latest academic and athletic achievements. We would usually spend about two hours in this conversation before we would begin to talk about business.

I knew he genuinely cared about me, about you, and about us. But I also learned a lot about sales management from him. An unhappy person does not make a very good sales representative. He understood that, and, if any of his people were unhappy about anything, he wanted to know about it. I quickly found that I could share any problems with him and that he would make a sincere effort to help me find solutions. He would often bring a new perspective to a dilemma and an answer would usually emerge during the course of our discussion. He often used a statement that I want you to always remember: "Work more on yourself than on your product or service." (My third letter will be totally devoted to applying these words to your sales career). He understood that you had to have product knowledge, but he also knew that without confidence, enthusiasm, and high self-esteem, no amount of expertise would lead you to the pleasant valley of success.

He shared motivational books with me and urged me to attend sales club and inspirational meetings as often as possible.

He had played football in his school days and compared selling to an athletic endeavor. He talked about how his coach would fire up the team before every game. He didn't make one speech to the team at the beginning of the year and then assume that the team would remain "up" for the rest of the season. His coach would inspire the team before the game, at half-time, during every game and would constantly motivate individual players along the sidelines throughout the game. He felt that this same process was necessary in the field of professional sales. And yet, many salespeople are hired, trained in the basics of their product or service, and are then cast into the harsh reality of the marketplace and warned to "Make quota or else."

He didn't believe in motivation by fear. He knew that each of his representatives had a family or other financial demands and that they had plenty of self-induced fears and pressure. He tried to relieve the stress by being a caring source of support rather than adding to it by being an overbearing monitor of our results.

He knew that if we liked ourselves as individuals and took pride in what we did, that we would be more successful. But, as I mentioned in the beginning of this letter, he did not just give advice. He took definite, positive steps to show each one of us that he truly cared.

When you were preparing to enroll in college, he knew that it would be a tough financial strain for me. He made me aware of a scholarship plan offered by the company based upon academic promise and the need of the employee. During one of our breakfast meetings, he brought all the papers for me to complete. He carefully helped me prepare every line to ensure the best possible chance for the application to be a success. He then pulled a letter from his coat, that he had written to attach to the application. It was a sincere, compelling list of reasons why, in his opinion, that I, as an employee, and you, as a student, would be outstanding recipients of this coveted scholarship. As you know, the story has a happy ending! You received the Foundation Scholarship for a period of three years and those funds made it possible for you to receive a first rate college education. How could I do anything less than give my very best to the company and to him as my supervisor. He cared. He said it and he showed it. I responded with the greatest possible effort, and in doing so, I was more successful as a salesperson and his success as a manager was also enhanced.

I have told you about his personal concerns for me and for what was important in my life. But he didn't make those gestures just toward me. He did them for every member of his regional sales team. That is why we were a family. You will come to understand someday that everyone wants to "belong". We all want to be accepted and to be part of something. Unfortunately, if something positive doesn't attract us, then we tend to gravitate toward something negative to fulfill our need to be okay with somebody. That is why I have always cautioned you about who you "hung around with". Peer pressure can be a highly negative force. It can also be a strong motivating, positive force. My sales manager understood this and created an environment designed to be a positive influence on all of us.

Our semi-annual meetings were almost like a revival. We would all leave those meetings convinced we could conquer the world. In hindsight, his methodology was both simple and ingenious. He did not lecture. He would select different salespeople in advance to make a brief presentation on something they had accomplished. This was an ego satisfying experience for the presenter and made the listeners realize that they were hearing a report from the firing line instead of theoretical suggestions prepared by ivory tower residents.

By comparison, many of my competitors would tell horror stories about their periodic sales meetings. There would be no advance agenda and the meetings would not follow a set schedule. As a result, the meetings would run on and on, causing the salespeople to resent the meetings and feel like they were a terrible waste of their time.

There were no corporate secrets in my company.

Our manager would begin the sales meetings with a brief update and would then take questions on any aspect of our company's activities. He made each of us feel that we were partners with upper management and that our job was as important as that of any employee in the organization.

He would then ask if there were any problems that anyone had which could be shared with the group. Next, he would encourage a lively discussion of the problem hoping a solution would emerge. This process would help us all in case we encountered a similar problem in the future. He could have dealt with the problem privately but that would have deprived the rest of the group from being exposed to both the problem and the process of arriving at a solution.

Following a discussion of problems, we would move into the presentations by various representatives. Everyone would put great effort into making the best possible presentation because they knew our manager had placed great trust in them. The fact that the presentations were rotated made everyone feel a part of the process and furthered the feeling of family he was striving to create. The methods he used to conduct these meetings were just another way in which he backed up his words by showing that he cared.

He also understood that "little things mean a lot", a phrase he repeated constantly. He had a favorite story, which I heard him tell many times, to illustrate the importance of doing the little things for both clients and fellow employees. He said an elderly aunt of his, who lived in a small southern town, once told him that most men failed to understand something very important about their relationship with their wives. Men would work hard to buy a nice home for their family, feed and properly clothe that family, and to provide a quality education for their children. But, the aunt said, "Rightly or wrongly, those things would not make a wife love a husband more. Why? Because rightly or wrongly, this is what every husband was supposed to do or, at the least, was expected to do." The acts that really caused love to deepen and that created idyllic, long lasting relationships, were "the little things" which were not what every good husband was supposed to do. It wasn't the husband who remembered to send flowers on an anniversary who was the hero, but the husband who sent flowers when there was no special occasion.

My sales manager would say that his aunt was a great sales manager although she had never been in sales or in management. He told me that he learned more about sales from her and that one, simple story than from all his professors or his managers. Whether dealing with clients or in managing salespeople, he always looked for the "little things" that he could do or say to endear himself and to leave a lasting impression. It worked for him in managing his sales force and it worked for those of us who took the time and trouble to apply this lesson to our client relationships. "Our employees expect us to support them with good products and support", he would say. "They feel that the company is supposed to do that and they expect it. My job as sales manager is to find the little things that we are not supposed to do as a company and to do them anyway." He felt that this would generate loyalty and improve performance, and he was right.

Clients are the same way. They expect you to have a good product and to provide them with good service. Most of your competitors will do the same. What will set you apart is the attention to the "little things" which show you care.

I have mentioned a few of the "little things" I tried to do such as sending regular communications to clients, remembering them on special occasions, being especially attuned to the accomplishments of their family members, and supporting them in times of trouble or tragedy. In simple terms, just be conscious of each of them as human beings and think about ways to make their lives more fun, more interesting and more rewarding. Most importantly, take action! Do not think fondly of a client because of something you see which reminds you of them, and then do nothing. If an event causes you to think of them, drop a note and share with them your reaction. They will know you cared enough not only to think of them, but to act on that thought and they will love you for it!

Another important way to express love is by sharing

your blessings. There are three distinct ways for you to experience sharing the joy of your blessings. The first way is to send out good feelings by being friendly and courteous to those around you and by emanating a positive attitude.

Good feelings have an electricity about them. Generate as much of that kind of energy as possible. Salesmen, by definition, must be optimists. They must expect the best and generate that positive attitude to their customers, their fellow workers, their competitors, and everyone with whom they come into contact.

By comparison, I have always felt managers must, by definition, be pessimists. They must expect the worst and be prepared for it. If the worst occurs, they can deal with it. If not, then they have the opportunity to enjoy the better than expected results. Having always been a natural optimist, it was easier for me to function as a salesman, than as a manager.

Enjoy being a salesman. Enjoy being an optimist. Do everything you possibly can to make other people feel better. Look for opportunities; be conscious of opportunities and take advantage of them when they appear. Let it be obvious by your actions that you have been blessed with success and that you want to spread that success to others.

If you become a manager then accept the obligations that go with that position. Prepare for the worst, but once you are prepared, then be a source of inspiration for the salespeople working for you. Help them be the optimists that they need to be.

The second thing you should do to share your blessings is to give away a portion of what you earn. I think the specific causes to which one contributes are less important than the fact that we are willing to give. As you know, I keep a mustard seed on my dresser at home. Many times I prayed to have the strength of that mustard seed which would enable me to follow its path and grow from my humble beginnings into something large and healthy. There have been a number of occasions when I was down to my last few dollars. At the time, when it seemed most foolish to give, I would seek out a cause and give some portion of what I had left. In the early days when I first began to sell, times were very difficult. These contributions came not just from my heart, but from the very depths of my soul. I tried to find joy and confidence in the realization that no matter how difficult the times seemed, or how insurmountable my problems appeared, there were many other people with greater problems. By the simple act of giving, I would always gain confidence and a sudden insight would almost always follow. The insight might be an idea for the next presentation I was making, or a strange inner feeling that I call someone I had not planned to call on that day. The results became uncanny. The act of faith on my part, would open up a channel in nature itself that would guide me in the right direction to make the next sale and keep me on the road to greater success.

I found that giving anonymously was far more rewarding than giving publicly. I never passed a beggar without at least dropping a few coins into his outstretched hand. I would read a sad story in the newspaper and then send a small contribution in an envelope with no return address. These gestures would always leave me feeling good about myself and that increased self-esteem and confidence would translate into more sales. You should never give to impress someone else with your kindness or generosity. However, I think it is perfectly alright to give in hopes that your kindness will be rewarded by the success that comes from feeling better about yourself.

Making monetary contributions is but one way to share your blessings, but it is an important part of the process of lining yourself up with the forces of nature which will seek you out and deliver success to your doorstep.

Thirdly, you should give graciously of your time. I was always actively involved in sales organizations. I found opportunities to help those who were struggling to achieve success in their selling careers. Many people fought depression, alcoholism, unhappiness at home, or tragedies in their own lives that would temporarily derail their careers, or at times threaten to not only ruin their careers, but their lives. I always tried to go out of my way to help these people. In time, I found that as I would help one person, they would say something to another person who would then come to me with their troubles.

I also became heavily involved with Reach For Recovery, an organization created to help women recovering from breast cancer. This was my special cause and became a very important part of my life. I was never more rewarded in my life than in those times when I could provide hope and encouragement to a woman with whom I had so much in common. I never felt put upon and deemed it an honor when someone would ask me to help them. I encourage you to seek out these kinds of opportunities because of the great joy they will bring you.

It is important to separate the differences in contributing your money from contributing your time or, what is more appropriately described as yourself, to another person or a cause. It is an impersonal act to contribute money to a cause. However, nothing is more personal than the human act of reaching out to another who is hurting. This is why you will find a different kind of reaction within yourself to these kinds of personal acts. Many people contribute money to causes and feel they have done their part and can leave the good works to others. It has been my experience that if you want to maximize the blessings of nature in a bountiful way, you can't just drop bills or coins into the collection plate. You must also become an active participant in helping those who are in need of your personal touch.

There is more to being happy and fulfilled than just achieving financial success. Woodrow Wilson said it beautifully, *"No thoughtful man ever came to the end of his life, and had time and a little space of calm from which to look back upon it, who did not know and acknowledge that it was what he had done unselfishly and for others, and nothing else that satisfied him in the retrospect..."* It is important for you to learn that the concept of sharing love, sharing feelings, and sharing your blessings with others will not only make you more successful but will enrich your life.

All my love,
Mother

Chapter Three

BREATHING

*"One of the greatest necessities in America
is to discover creative solitude."*
— CARL SANDBURG

Dear Son,

Here is the second installment which will hopefully
guide you on the road to a successful career. Lesson
Number Two is one word: *Breathe.* I hope you are not
disappointed to find that my second secret is something that we all do just to continue to live. However,
that is not the kind of involuntary breathing to which I
am referring.

I originally intended for this to be my first letter,

but I was afraid that you would not find it substantial enough and would not take my advice seriously. Hopefully, the first lesson has demonstrated that I do have valuable experience and ideas from which you can benefit. Please take this second letter seriously. There are many physical and mental benefits to be derived from proper breathing. I want to focus on two.

First, proper breathing will relieve stress and tension. I cannot recall the many times that one, two, or three deep breaths helped me through a crisis. I would be sitting in an office, especially when I first began, gripped by fear and panic. There were times early on when I would literally get up and walk out of an office and stand in the fresh air gasping for breath. I learned quickly that a few deep breaths would give me not only renewed strength, but the confidence I needed to proceed.

Second, if you learn to breathe properly, you can learn to relax. You will then find that in a relaxed state, your mind will open and become receptive to insight and inspiration.

I found that the best way to breathe was to close my eyes, tilt my head backwards and expand my navel outward as far as it would go, taking in as much air as possible. I would repeat the word "relax" as I did so. Within a few moments, no matter how frightened I might have been, I would feel an uncanny sense of well being come over my body. The feeling would begin at the top of my head and flow freely throughout my body. It was almost like an electrical current that would exit my fingers and the ends of my toes, leaving me confident, invigorated, and refreshed.

Proper breathing is an acquired skill which can be practiced like any other skill. The more you do it, the better you will get. But remember, as with all things, only perfect practice will create perfection. If you breathe casually, without concentrating on the act of what you are doing, you will derive minimum benefit. Feel your abdomen expand, feel it contract. Feel the air come in through your nostrils as you inhale and feel the contraction in your abdomen as you exhale. Concentrate on the sensation of relaxation taking over your body from the top of your head to the tips of your fingers and toes as you slowly and fully exhale. Below is an excerpt from <u>Yoga For Americans</u> written in 1959, by Indra Devi which describes in simple terms, the art of breathing:

"Inhalation is done in one smooth continuous flow just as one might pour water in filling a glass. First the bottom is filled, then the middle, and finally the upper portion. But the process itself — pouring in order to fill the entire glass — is an uninterrupted one. Just so is the air taken in, in one uninterrupted inhalation, while the lungs fill with air; just so is the air expelled until the lungs are empty. But you must do it slowly and in a most relaxed manner. No effort or strain should ever be exerted. This is very important. Keep mouth closed.

You then become aware of the function of your own diaphragm. You expand the flanks when inhaling and contract them when exhaling. The lower part of the rib cage naturally expands first when you breathe in and is compressed last when you let the air out. This too should be done gently, without any force or strain. The chest remains motionless and passive during the entire process of respiration. Only the ribs expand during inhalation and contract during exhalation, accordion-fashion. To use force during inhalation is completely wrong. One should do it with ease, without tension or strain whatever. In deep breathing, exhalation is as important as inhalation because it eliminates poisonous matter. The lower part of our lungs seldom are sufficiently emptied, and tend to accumulate air saturated with waste products, for with ordinary breathing we never expel enough of the carbon dioxide our system throws off even if we do inhale enough oxygen. If, on the other hand, the lower part of the lungs are properly expanded and contracted, the circulation in the liver and spleen, which are thus "massaged" by the diaphragm, are greatly benefitted."

I suggest you buy this book, which has been one of my prized possessions and a great asset on my road to success, and practice many of the simple exercises described in the book. Concentrate on mastering proper breathing techniques. Remember, only perfect practice will create perfection. Read the paragraph I have quoted above, over and over. Work constantly to perfect the manner and style of your breathing. You will be better able to deal with stressful situations, and you will also find your mind more receptive to the kinds of thoughts and feelings which will guide you to your greater purpose in life. I will tell you more about how to use breathing to relax and open your mind in my next letter. The goal setting and realization procedures described in my next letter are far more likely to be successful if you master proper breathing.

Learning to breathe in a time of crisis or even in a situation of mild pressure will stand you in good stead throughout your career. Once you develop the habit of taking smooth, deep breaths in any difficult moment, you will find that proper breathing will contribute to good posture. In turn, the proper posture will create an aura of confidence about you which other people will notice.

I find that anytime I am feeling defeated or temporarily depressed, I can throw my shoulders back, stretch to my full height, take a few deep breaths and instantaneously feel a burst of confidence. I stress the importance of posture, not only for the impression it gives other people, but because of the way you feel. In the past, I have been sitting in an office waiting on an appointment and feeling down or sorry for myself. I will suddenly realize that I am in a slouched position, almost cowering in my chair. Not only will I take the breaths as described earlier, but I will immediately straighten up in my chair, throw my shoulders back and look confident, regardless of how I might feel at the moment. My experience has been that the very act of improving my posture along with the proper breathing, renews my enthusiasm. You may be skeptical of the idea that a few breaths and a straightened posture can have a positive impact on your mental state. Trust me. Try it. You will be absolutely amazed, as I have come to be, of the impact that these two things can have on your overall mental well being.

You will find, that as you become better at breathing, you will do much of the right kind of breathing unconsciously. I would find myself driving from one appointment to another taking deep breaths and feeling my hand relax on the steering wheel. There is no substitute for the refreshing, invigorating input of a few solid, deep breaths. As I go forward in these letters, I will give you more specific ideas regarding the things you need to do to be a successful salesperson. However, none will be more important than this simple process. Take seriously the act of breathing and learn to appreciate the divinely inspired feeling of self assurance which comes over you when you breathe properly.

All my love,
Mother

Chapter Four

WORK MORE ON YOURSELF
THAN ON YOUR PRODUCT

*"We meet ourselves time and again
in a thousand disguises on the path of life.*

— CARL JUNG

Dear Son,

As promised in my first letter, this third lesson will help you learn to work more on yourself than on your product or service. The majority of people spend a lot of time trying to understand the product or service they sell, but very little time on understanding the salesperson — themselves.

I began asking other salespeople, both among my

competitors and in other fields of specialty, what their goals were. In five years of inquiry, I found only three salespeople who had written, specific goals about the things that they wanted to accomplish. You may find that hard to believe, but it is true. In almost every case, sales representatives were assigned quotas by their company, or sales manager, or someone who would benefit from their success. After constant exposure to these situations, I came to a compelling conclusion. For goals to be effective, they must be personal; they must be your own goals. They cannot be goals passed down from a supervisor or directed from impersonal corporate policy makers.

I also learned that the process of defining goals is extremely difficult but one that is essential to meaningful success. Implementing a goal is actually the easier part of the process. If you are fortunate enough to discover a goal which thoroughly motivates your every act, then the steps to achieving that goal become virtually automatic. Therefore, there are two parts to this lesson. The first is to learn how to set goals, and the second is how to implement them.

I am going to discuss the two parts of the process in reverse order. Let me begin with the easy part — what to do once you have a goal. From there we will go into the hard part, understanding yourself well enough to truly realize what your goals are.

Once you have arrived at a goal for yourself, do the following:

1. Write it down. Do this in concise, plain language and use the present tense. To use a simple example: I am writing one letter per week to my active clients, and I am opening one new account per week. Then not only read this written statement aloud to yourself at least twice a day, but also say it over and over to yourself throughout the day. As you are waiting for an appointment, repeat the statement constantly to yourself. Learn to visualize the words on a giant screen written in different colors and in different types of script. It is also important that you practice the experience of how you will feel when the goal has been accomplished. If your goal is to receive an award, then practice the acceptance speech. Feel the chill bumps crawl along your skin as the audience rises to applaud you. Hear the shouts of "Bravo!" as you bask in the glow of your accomplishment. Don't just dream, but put yourself in the dream and experience through all your senses how you will feel when the dream is a reality.

2. State a date certain for the achievement of your goal. For example, I am driving a new, red Cadillac on June 1, 19_ as a result of my efforts to open one new account per week. This is an important part of the process. Your mind reacts best to something definite rather than something vague. By providing a date certain for achieving your goals, you will provide a greater channel through which your efforts can be directed.

3. Write down all the reasons why your goal will become a reality. This step is critical in determining the reality of your objective. If you are 25 years old and stand 5'10" tall, a goal to be 6'4" is not grounded in reality. That is an extreme example but you must grasp the point that every goal must be realistic. If you are unable to list any specific reasons why a goal will be realized, then you have just failed the all important reality check and you need to renew your search for a goal or goals. On the positive side, this listing will encourage you and convince you that the achievement of your goal is a realistic expectation.

4. Make a written list of everything you will have to do to achieve your goal. This is also a reality check. I discovered that several goals which I had established for myself would not pass this test. Be honest in making this list. I know you hate cold weather. If your goal is to be an Alpine skier, then you would have to spend a lot of time on windy ski slopes. I doubt that you would be willing to pay that price even for an Olympic gold medal. Again, use that extreme example as a barometer when evaluating your willingness to do whatever it takes to reach your goal. If you won't pay whatever price is required, then you have to select a new objective which requires you to do that which you are both willing and able to do.

There, that is it, or at least that was enough for me. Write down your goals, stipulate a specific time for their realization, list the reasons why you expect to reach the goals and what you will have to do to get there. That is a simple four step formula which worked time and again for me.

Now for the much harder part — deciding what goals are most important to you. A very few lucky individuals seem to be born knowing what they want. You've known a few people like that. At an early age, you ask them what they want to be and with no hesitation, they blurt right out "an airline pilot" or "a doctor" or whatever. Driven by their never wavering aim toward a clear objective, their life becomes like a construction project following a carefully drawn blueprint. Others are fortunate to discover their calling in life due to the inspiration of a teacher, exposure to a role model, or from reading a moving piece of literature. Maybe the most fortunate of all are those who are divinely inspired. You've known ministers or social workers who feel they are responding to a particular moment when in a dream or vision, they feel the "call" to pursue their life's work. But what of the rest of us? I am convinced that a meaningful, significant goal can be discovered in the life of every individual.

In my last letter, I discussed in detail the importance of learning how to breathe properly. By mastering this skill, you will learn how to breathe in a way that will allow you to relieve the stress of tense situations. Proper breathing will also allow you to relax and in a state of relaxation, to explore your inner self. It is now time to combine the process of proper breathing and induced relaxation in an effort to discover those things which mean the most to you and can become the motivating force, or forces, in your life.

Let me illustrate by telling you a story of someone I met during one of the sales meetings I attended. As I told you, my sales manager urged me to join sales clubs and to constantly spend time in the company of motivated, successful sales people. Well, at one of the luncheon meetings, I found myself sitting next to a securities salesman who worked for one of the major New York Stock Exchange firms. We will call him Larry. We began a conversation comparing notes about our respective industries. I would see him at various functions, and our relationship grew as we began to share our mutual interest in improving our professional selling skills. Larry shared with me the process he used to discover goals that motivated him to achieve tremendous success in his field. He was the leading producer in the entire region for his company. He had overcome many obstacles along the way to finding both financial success and great self satisfaction.

Larry was born in a small town in Arkansas. His parents were divorced when he was only three and he never knew his father, who left for California after the divorce and was killed a few years later in an automobile accident. He was the youngest of three boys. His oldest brother was killed in an accident involving heavy equipment on a construction site. The second brother was arrested repeatedly as a juvenile and died in prison. His mother worked as a waitress, barely making ends meet and had a steady succession of men in her life, none of whom ever married her and assumed the role of a father figure for Larry. His mother drank heavily and never gave him any encouragement to seek a better life for himself.

One day, as a frustrated, non-driven teenager, he dropped out of school and joined the Army. This was after World War II and before the Korean War, but he was sent overseas, as was the case with so many American servicemen after World War II, to keep peace in the world. At this point, his life began to change and to move in a positive direction. I don't remember many of his exact words in relaying the story of his experiences to me, but I do remember the lessons Larry learned and was kind enough to pass on to me.

He shared a barracks with a young man from New York who hated being in the military. Apparently, this individual had been drafted into the service and counted the days carefully until he would be free of his military obligation and could return home and begin the pursuit of fame and fortune. However, he was determined not to waste his time and set about filling any extra hours he had in the most constructive way possible. Let's call him Tom. Well, Larry and Tom found themselves spending a lot of time together discussing, among other things, what they would do when their military days were behind them. Unlike Larry, Tom came from a loving, supportive family. His parents and other relatives were successful and had raised him to believe that he could do anything he set his mind to accomplish. This in itself was a valuable lesson for Larry to learn. He had never thought about the possibility of taking control of his own life and rising above his humble station in life. Tom had written goals for himself as to how much money he would make, about the kind of person he would marry and the exact kind of house they would live in. He had many details of his future life reduced to writing including a time frame for their accomplishment. Virtually all of Tom's goals later came true and most were accomplished within the time expectations he had set forth. Thus, Larry learned the first two lessons in my four step process; write down specific goals, and set a definite time for their achievement.

However, there was still one major problem for Tom and in some ways, the most important lesson of all was still to come for Larry. During their conversations, the initially skeptical Larry would tell Tom, "Okay great, you're going to make all this money and have all those things, but you still haven't told me <u>how</u> you are going to make all this money." Tom did not have an answer when the two began to talk. However, he did have a process for finding an answer. The process, which was very simple, worked for Tom, and Larry was smart enough to learn from Tom and duplicate the process. I hopefully, have also put much of what I learned from Larry into practice in my own life. First, he made a list of all his strengths and the resources he had to call upon. For example, he had a caring family, had been fortunate enough to receive a solid education, had been exposed to Germany as a result of his Army experience, and had no wife nor children to take care of at this point which he felt made it easier for him to take risks. I have listed just a few of the items he put on his list to give you a flavor for the process.

The list Tom made was a statement on his part, of the reasons why his goal or goals would become a reality. He had now taken three of the four steps I listed earlier:

1. He wrote down his goals. Of course, at this point, he wrote down the results he wanted (a car, house, etc.) and not what he was going to do to achieve these things. This was to come later. It is important to notice that he began in pursuit of the "what" before he finally knew the "how".

2. He set a date certain for achievement of his objectives.

3. He made a list of reasons why his goals would become reality.

Tom began with a theory that every individual had special skills and could prosper if they could just discover, harness, and develop those unique talents. He viewed the process more as an inner search of discovery than one of mastering an outside force. He would lie on his bunk or on the grass outside the barracks with his eyes closed, taking slow, deep breaths. His objective was to achieve a state of total relaxation so his "real self" could emerge. This was not something he did casually or periodically. He devoted some time every day to this process. He combined the importance of disciplined breathing with the process of coming to know himself. He sincerely believed that a plan for his life would reveal itself through this simple program of self analysis. He was right. It worked! He then had the "how" that would be the vehicle for making all the "whats" come true. He then could take step four, making a written list of everything he would have to do to achieve his goals.

Tom became one of the most successful exporters in the United States. He did not like the Army, but he turned the time that he spent in the military into a positive experience. He learned to speak German and correctly predicted that the energy and skill of the German people would permit them to rebuild their country and their economy. He made many friends during his Army stint and they became the cornerstone of his success.

Larry described to me the conversation the two had when Tom realized that he had found himself and knew what he would do with his life. Larry walked into the barracks and was grabbed by an excited, exuberant Tom. "Larry, Larry, I've got it!" he shouted. "The idea has been taking shape for weeks but today, while I was stretched out on the bunk, the whole plan just fell into place." Tom proceeded to describe his overall business plan which, with only minor adjustments, became a hugely successful business. He studied the German people. He studied their economic recovery plan. He made contacts within the government and in the private sector. He discovered that he had a gift for steering his way through the bureaucratic world of exporting. He came to understand what he was good at by coming to know himself. He developed a plan which took advantage of his skills. He then executed his plan and in time, with great perseverance, he became a huge success.

Larry followed the system. He learned to put himself into a state of relaxation, allowing his mind to wander and to dream. He also made a list of his strengths and resources both of which numbered far less than Tom's. However, that is part of the reality check. Don't try to be someone else. Evaluate your own situation and determine your own strengths and resources. Be honest in looking at your shortcomings. Investigate your likes, your dislikes, your feelings, and your desires.

Larry wasn't as smart as Tom. He didn't have as much education and he didn't have strong family support. But he loved people and thoroughly enjoyed the process of selling. He also had a driving ambition to make money. He needed to find something where he could sell, make money, and have no initial capital investment. Eventually, he found his way into the brokerage business, and, as they say, "The rest is history."

From the joint experience of Tom and Larry, I learned to evaluate my strengths and weaknesses and to breathe and relax in order to quietly examine my inner self. Through this process, I came to discover my calling as a salesperson and to develop a plan for achieving both satisfaction and the material things I dreamed of having.

I am enclosing my original copy of Napoleon Hill's classic book, <u>Think and Grow Rich</u>. As you can see, the pages are graying and the underlined phrases, sentences, and paragraphs, are numerous throughout the book. I have spent many hours studying this book and strongly recommend that you do the same.[1]

I have tried to tell you how to identify and then reach the one, two, or few major goals in your life. However, I

---

[1] Author's Note": It is interesting to note that an entire industry has cropped up around motivational books, tapes, etc., since <u>Think and Grow Rich</u> was first published. However, my mother always felt, and conveyed to me in later years, that <u>Think and Grow Rich</u> was the genesis for the entire industry. She also felt that virtually every business lesson one needed to learn about being a success could be gleaned from the pages of this masterpiece.

don't want to fail to stress the importance of having smaller goals which motivate you on a daily basis. Generally, the all encompassing life goals must be discovered as opposed to being created. By coming to know yourself, you must open yourself to receive this information as both Larry and Tom learned to do. Don't try to force these broad goals into your psyche. Pave the way for their entrance and then stand aside and be receptive.

We are told in <u>Think and Grow Rich</u> that we must have a "burning desire" to achieve a definite result. But what if you don't have such a "burning desire" and have been unable to either create one or discover one? Then you must develop small, interim goals and use them as motivation while continuing to open yourself to the possibility of discovering your "burning desire." Too many people give up on using goals in any form because they are unable to find a single driving force in their life. Don't follow that pattern.

My goal setting process went through a number of stages. One of my earliest goals was to find a job to support you and me. I visualized specifically, the kind of job it would be complete with an income level. I once read that philosophy usually flourishes in societies where there is a great deal of leisure time. This is no doubt true. When one is struggling to provide essentials, there is little time for contemplation. However, no matter how busy, how stressed, or how pushed, I always allowed some time to think about where I wanted to go, what it would take to get there, and what it would be like when I arrived.

After settling on sales as my chosen profession, one of my next goals was to develop the self-confidence which would allow my selling skills to grow and flourish. I had lists of things to do to achieve this goal. Again, I was specific as to duties, time frame, and income level. My next goal was to find a more financially rewarding opportunity. One of my continuous goals, which again overlapped with several others, was to see you complete your education. This was also accomplished.

In addition to these goals, I would set daily, weekly, and monthly goals for myself. Some were as simple as the number of calls I would make or the number of letters I would write. No matter how simple or short-term, I still followed the four step procedure:

1. **Write it down**

2. **Specify a time for accomplishment of the goal.**

3. **List the reasons why you expect the goal to be reached.**

4. **List exactly what you will have to do to achieve the goal.**

These kinds of very specific, interim goals serve as practice while waiting for the emergence of a life dominating, all consuming, almost obsessive "definite result". As I indicated, you can't force this emergence. You can only prepare yourself for it. This is critical for you to understand.

You can achieve substantial sales success and lead a highly enjoyable and rewarding life without ever discovering this "obsession". Many people spend a lifetime without ever seeking to know themselves and thus opening the channel to the possibility of discovering their "primary goal". However, many others spend their lives futilely trying to convince themselves that they have found "it". When the forced fit begins to pinch, they rebel by changing careers, turning to alcohol or elsewhere for relief, and usually blame others for their misery. These people never understand the importance of secondary or interim goals and consider themselves failures because they lack an overriding goal in life. Don't fall into either of these traps.

Winston Churchill is often cited as an example of someone with an overriding goal. In his case, it was the defeat of Hitler and the Nazi menace. But, what if Hitler had never taken power or attempted to expand beyond Germany's existing borders? Churchill was not born wanting to defeat Hitler. The situation came to Churchill, and he responded because he was prepared. He was open to receive what proved to be a call to his destiny. Interestingly enough, even before the close of the war, British voters chose to replace Churchill, feeling that approaching peacetime called for different leadership.

Always prepare yourself and be open to the entrance of the grand design for your life. In the meantime, use your time wisely. Become proficient at setting interim goals. Recognize their importance and do everything possible to make each one a reality.

There is one more part of this critical lesson for you to learn. It took me a long time to realize that there is a difference between goals and priorities. It is critical that you understand the distinction and at all times know what your goals are as well as what your priorities are and that you resolve any conflicts between the two. Let me give you an example. Assume that your goal is to be the number one salesperson in your office for the coming year which would mean total annual production of x amount. Let's assume further that in order to reach that goal, you would have to double your current production. This would mean that you would need to increase your working hours by a substantial percentage and complete a long list of other things which you know would be required in order to reach this goal. Let's then assume further that your introspection has convinced you that the most important thing in your life is spending time with your family. This is truly your number one priority. You can see the obvious conflict between this goal and your real priority. I think this is an often misunderstood difficulty that individuals have in successfully setting goals for themselves. The average individual tends to have fantasies or unrealistic dreams rather than goals. I wrote earlier to you about making reality checks. The additional reality check of measuring each goal against your true priorities in life is as critical as any other.

It is also important to know that just as our goals can change so can our priorities. When I went through a period of major illness in my life, my first priority became my health, and doing everything that was necessary to get well. I realized that unless I got well, there would be no other priorities in my life, nor could any other goals be realized. Once I passed the critical phase and began to enjoy the great vigor that comes with good health, I was able to reorder my priorities. Just as with goals, priorities must be your own. If you allow other people to set goals for you, you do not have a true commitment to make those goals a reality. This is even more true with priorities in your life. Priorities are bigger than specific goals and transcend the ideas embodied in particular goals. It is critical that each goal you set for yourself, no matter how large or small, or how short-term or long term, be measured against your true priorities.

Always stress working to know yourself better and strive to improve yourself. One of the exciting things about this process is that it never ends. As long as you live, you have the opportunity to explore and to improve. Let me give you a short list of additional, specific things I have done in the constant quest for self-improvement:

1. Read biographies of great people. You have always been a reader, but take great care as to what you read. The things you read find crevices within your mind and become attached to you for life. They have unseen and unknown influences on your performance. Therefore, take great care as to what you give an opportunity to become a part of your subconscious recollections.

2. Have firm values. Treasure integrity above all. It is vital that you form a firm base founded in integrity. Throughout your life as a salesperson, you will face temptations. You must have a core of integrity which is unyielding to those temptations. Never, under any circumstances, compromise your integrity. No sale is worth the damage it will do to your reputation or self-esteem.

3. Seek out great sellers of products or services. I am sure that you have heard the old cliche that one rotten apple will ruin the whole barrel. In our society, that tends to happen more than you might think. We need to associate with people who are successful and help them pull us up. No matter how strong you are, if you associate with negative talkers and negative thinkers, or people who are constantly complaining, you will find yourself affected by their input. I have never met a consistent top salesman who had a bad attitude. You can also model yourself after the success of another person. Larry learned from Tom, and I, in turn, learned from Larry. Find someone in your field whom you admire and respect. Get to know them. You will find that most salespeople are willing to share their secrets. Just as I take pride in these letters, most salespeople will take great pride in their successes and great joy in sharing them. Take advantage of these opportunities.

4. Make an honest appraisal of yourself. List your strengths and weaknesses. Be honest in compiling the list. Ask people you know well to help you with this input. Make a list of those things you want to change. Make a second list of what you will have to do to bring about the changes. Set a time frame for making the change a reality. Then take action. Do it! Make the improvements you know you need to make. In the meantime, once you know what your strengths are, try to put yourself in situations where you can maximize those things which you do best.

5. Stay fit. This is something that I don't have to stress to you because you have always tried to workout and take care of yourself. You don't smoke and be sure you never start. Drink only moderately and never drink to excess around clients or even friends which would cause your reputation to suffer. You cannot concentrate on improving yourself or even knowing yourself if you don't feel well.

6. Learn to breathe, relax and to prepare yourself for the grand design to enter your life. Remember, the compelling life mission kind of goal is not something you can create. It is something you must allow to emerge. Once you have achieved a comfortable state of relaxation, let your inner mind wander. Listen to your internal conversation. As you practice achieving a calm state of relaxation, you will find your intuition becoming more active. If you just listen it will begin to guide you. There are great discoveries to be made by exploring your own inner self and by allowing your intuition to play a key role in planning your future. I realize that I am repeating my earlier suggestion about breathing, but I cannot overemphasize the importance of learning to breathe properly.

I don't want you to misunderstand the need to know your product or service. You should spend the necessary time to master the product or service you are selling. This can usually be done in a relatively short period of time. Updates, in the form of continuing education, can keep you abreast of everything you need to know. However, the process of self-knowledge and self-improvement is a life long study which will be personally fulfilling as well as beneficial in terms of career advancement. Bon voyage!

All my love,
Mother

Chapter Five

STUDY PEOPLE

"Whenever two people meet
there are really six people present.
There is each man as he sees himself,
each man as the other person sees him,
and each man as he really is."

— WILLIAM JAMES

Dear Son,

If you take seriously the idea of studying people, you will augment your chances of being successful, and you will have a lot more fun in life. The vast majority of people are kind, caring, gracious, and a delight to know. Don't be dissuaded from this view by the few exceptions you'll meet in your career. It is far more rewarding to assume that someone is a "good person" until they prove to be otherwise than to take the opposite approach. In other words, take a positive approach to everyone you meet. This is an important rule to accept before beginning the process of studying an individual. If you begin with a negative feeling toward the person, or worse yet, towards people in general, you will find that most of the bad things come true. If you are predisposed to finding negatives, your initial feelings will become a self fulfilling prophecy. It is critical that you start from the right frame of mind in your approach to studying people. Once you have accepted the positive premise, you can begin the specific steps in the process.

I

Learn everything possible about the people you are trying to do business with.

Please understand the two benefits to be derived from this process. First, you will know their interests, their likes and dislikes, and what is important in their life. This will aid you in creating rapport with each individual and that will result in sales. Second, and you may be surprised at this, they will not feel intruded upon in any way but will be complimented that you cared enough to do the research and that will also result in more sales. One of my later letters will suggest that you strive to be different. The act of caring enough to learn all you can about your prospects and clients will, in and of itself, make you different.

II

Use every possible source to gather information about your subject.

It isn't enough to decide you want to know all you can know about someone. You must have a systematic plan for gathering the information. My plan was simple. I asked everyone who knew a particular person, to tell me everything that they knew about that person. I then learned as much as possible by speaking directly to the person I was studying. Then, and this is critical, I would write down everything I learned in a readily accessible format. Let me elaborate.

I would ask a secretary or receptionist for information. I would politely push for as much information as they seemed willing to share. Some were reluctant and afraid they would get into trouble if they talked too much. I never pushed. At the slightest hint of hesitation, I would back off. My questions were always casual. I stressed that the more I knew about the boss, the better I would be able to serve his needs. Most never hesitated to share both general and specific information.

I usually began with specific questions, but ones that would not seem intrusive or provocative. For example, I would say, "It has always been my practice to send birthday cards to all of my clients. When is Mr. X's birthday?" They almost always told me the answer to that question and I would be on my way with an important piece of information. Many of my competitors failed to realize the importance of developing a good relationship with the secretaries and receptionists. That was a terrible mistake. Never, ever, underestimate the importance of cultivating these people. They will appreciate your courtesy and will in almost every case, respond favorably. They can not only provide you with valuable information, but can also give you access to the boss while making it difficult for the competition.

As I got to know the support personnel better, I would open up more, telling them exactly what I was trying to accomplish. It was important to stress that by knowing more about their boss, I could do a better job for him. Most accepted the obvious truth of this and told me virtually everything I wanted to know.

I would expand my base of information by talking to business or social friends or acquaintances of my prospect. This I would do very carefully. I was not looking for specific information such as a birthday or names and ages of children. I was interested in general information about the kind of person they were. I might begin by saying to a colleague of Mr. X's that I had been in his office recently and was impressed by the friendly nature of his entire staff. Then I would ask, "He must be an awfully nice person to attract such good people. What is he really like?" This kind of general question, always preceded by a favorable comment, would usually elicit a lengthy response, telling me a lot of things I had not known before.

Notice a couple of important points. I never said anything negative about the person. On the contrary, I always led into my question with a specific, positive comment. In addition, my question was always broad and general and could never be interpreted as an intrusive inquiry into the details of the person's private life. This left the depth and degree of the response totally up to the individual with whom I was speaking.

III

Use a standardized form on which to record the information you gather.

You cannot possibly remember all the information you gather. Thus, it is critical to write it down in a readily accessible manner. When I first began the process of gathering information on clients and prospects, I used index cards which I kept in alphabetical order. However, this approach lacked organization and standardization. After several false starts, I developed my Personal Information Profile which I referred to as my PIP sheet. Below, I have set out the actual PIP sheet that I used:

PERSONAL INFORMATION PROFILE

1. Name: _____

2. Address: (0) _____

   (H) _____

3. Phone: (0) _____

   (H) _____

4. Name of Spouse: _____

   Anniversary: _____

   Employment: _____

   Charitable/Social Activities_____

   _____

   _____

5. Names/Ages of Children: _____

   _____

   _____

6. Nature of Practice: _____

   (This form was used in dealing with medical practitioners. It could be used for any industry or business.)

7. Birthday: _____

8. Name of High School: _____

9. Undergraduate School: _____

10. Medical School: _____

11. Internship: _____

12. Residency: _____

13. Military Service: _____

    Branch:_____

    Rank Achieved: _____

    Length of Service: _____

    Where Stationed:_____

14. Parent(s) Occupation(s): _____

15. Hometown: _____

16. Hobbies: _____

    (Include details as to how active the individual is, how important the hobby is in their life and show how accomplished they are.)

17. Organizational Activities: _____

    Service Clubs:_____

       Leadership Positions: _____

    Industry Groups: _____

       Leadership Positions: _____

    Charities:_____

       Leadership Positions: _____

18. Religious Affiliation:_____

       Leadership Positions _____

19. Political Affiliation:_____

20. Name of Office Manager: _____

21. Background Summary of Office Manager: _____

_____

_____

_____

_____

_____

_____

22. Names of Other Key Office Personnel: _____

23. Background Summary on Key Office Personnel:_____

_____

_____

_____

_____

24. Preferred Time to Accept Calls: _____

    To Schedule Office Visits: _____

25. Enjoyment of Work: _____

_____

_____

_____

_____

26. Name(s) of Best Friend(s): _____

    Nature of Relationship: _____

27. Personal Hero(s):_____

28. Major Goal in Life: _____

   (With some this will be difficult to determine because most won't have such a goal. Others will be very private about this information; however, if you can get this information, you will take a giant step toward developing a solid relationship with the client.)

29. Primary Accomplishments: _____

30. Disappointments or Tragedies: _____

31. Greatest Strengths:_____

32. Greatest Weaknesses:_____
   (The above two responses would be based on input received and on my own impressions.)

33. Pet Peeves: _____

34. Personal Habits: _____

   Drinker: _____ Smoker: _____

   Favorite Foods:_____

   Favorite Restaurants:_____

35. Medical Problems: _____

36. Type of Pet: _____

   Name of Pet: _____

37. Make of Automobile:_____

38. Relatives or close friends of the client who are competitors

   of mine: _____

39. Description of Items on Desk or Wall of Office:_____

   _____

_____

_____

_____

40. Anything unusual about literature in waiting room:_____

_____

_____

_____

41. Responds to Visual Aids: _____

_____

_____

_____

(This was based on my actual experience with the client and would reflect a description of what aids I used, the client's reaction, and the circumstances).

42. Miscellaneous Information:_____

_____

_____

_____

_____

(This served as a catch-all for any information acquired which did not fit into any of the previous headings.)

You can add to, delete from, or amend this form in any way you see fit, to match the business or industry of your clients. The key is to use some type of form which is standardized and which can be referred to readily. Continue to add information as you gather it, and always remember to review the form before every visit with the client. I also kept notes on each meeting, the product I presented, and the client's reaction, but those notes were kept in my call book and were not normally made a part of the PIP sheet.

IV

What you say to your customer isn't as important as what you hear.

Listen to what people say. Most salesmen are too busy talking and listening to themselves to take the time to listen to the customer. Most people will tell you what they really think and want if you will just give them your attention and listen. Most people also take offense when they sense that you are not listening to them. In the first place, it is rude and shows a lack of sincere interest. Secondly, it will lead to a tremendous waste of time because if you don't listen, you will wind up pursuing a lot of dead ends and spending unproductive time.

V

Learn to read what people mean, not just what they say.

Don't just listen to the words, but watch the expressions. Listen to the inflections, and interpret the gestures. Record your impressions and reflect on them later. You will find future meetings with that prospect far more productive. This is a tremendous art for you to master.

Emerson wrote, *"What you are speaks so loudly I can't hear what you are saying."* Study what people say and how they say it but also study what they do, how they move, and what other people think of them. Look for inconsistencies between their words and their actions. Strong messages emit from body movements. They may be saying no, but meaning yes, or saying yes, and really meaning no. If you have studied the art of body movement, eye contact, facial gestures, and voice inflection, you will be able to detect such subtle communications. Let me give you some of the specifics I have learned from many years of studying people:

a. If people say they will buy or use your product, but there is no enthusiasm or conviction in their voice, then don't go spend the money.

b. People who are interested will lean forward or toward you. Those who are not interested will tend to lean back or move away from you.

c. If people are genuinely interested, they will usually ask questions and the inflections in their voice will convey the degree of their commitment.

d. If people are tapping their feet, or strumming their fingers, you should stop your presentation, tell them you have the feeling that they are too busy to focus, and ask to reschedule another meeting in the future. They will either apologize and give you their attention, agree to reschedule, or tell you that they are not interested, which will save you a lot of time and wasted effort. When you know a prospect is distracted, don't forge ahead. You are wasting your time and offending them, if only subconsciously.

e. Always look people in the eye. This delivers a message of confidence and control. If a person refuses to return your eye contact, they are probably unreceptive to your presentation. However, there may be an exception to this suggestion. I have found that people who won't make eye contact are sometimes just shy or introverted. Thus, you will need to look for other signs to properly evaluate their level of interest.[2]

---

[2] Author's Note: Again, I think my mother was ahead of her time. She spent many hours talking to me about the observations discussed above. Unfortunately, until only recently did I understand the significance of her studies of body language. In the past few years, I have tried to take her studies and expand on them. The best book on the subject is Instant Rapport, by Michael Brooks published by Warner Books, 1989. She would have taken great delight in seeing her theory of studying body language evolve to the level of sophistication as described in Instant Rapport.

f. Folded arms generally mean the listener is not receptive to your presentation. You should read that signal, change directions, and try a different approach.

g. Do not touch someone until you have established that they welcome the touch. Some people like to be tapped on the arm, or have an arm thrown around their shoulders, or be hugged. They will respond favorably to physical contact. Those who do not like to be touched, will be repelled and become extremely defensive.

h. Raised eyebrows suggest that the listener is questioning what you are saying.

i. As indicated in one of my earlier letters, an erect posture generally reflects confidence, while a slumped bearing usually indicates a lack of confidence.

These are, of course, not absolutes. There will be exceptions to every rule. You will have to experiment, through trial and error, and reach workable conclusions. The guidelines set out above worked for me and will serve as a good starting point for you in exploring this fascinating area.

VI

Use the information you
have gathered wisely.

It is important that you be careful in the ways you use the personal information about an individual. It is acceptable to send birthday cards or other cards or letters which commemorate special occasions. It is also strongly recommended that you clip articles from the newspaper about your client or members of their family and send those articles along with a personal note.

However, if you have gathered personal background information about an individual, you cannot blurt out what you know. Obviously, as you get closer to people and your relationship deepens, they will be delighted to learn that you took the time and trouble to learn who they are and what they are all about. But in the beginning, you should work what you know into the conversation in the proper way. I was once told that a speaker should never tell a joke unless it is appropriate to the context of the overall presentation. I would give you the same advice in using the information you have gathered. For example, if you know the individual is planning a vacation to a specific destination to pursue their hobby, then do some research on the destination and work that into your conversation. "Dr. X, I understand that you are going on a fishing trip to Wherever, USA. I have never been there, but some of my friends went there last year and gave me a list of restaurants in the area. I jotted down the names of the restaurants for you along with a little background information which they were nice enough to share with me. I hope it makes your trip more enjoyable."

Another example: "Dr. Y, I was visiting with Dr. Z last week and he mentioned that you two are not only close friends but that your friendship goes all the way back to medical school. He is such a nice person and has been a wonderful supporter and client of mine. In the midst of telling me how much respect he has for you, he shared with me the fact that you are heavily involved in ABC Charity. The ABC Group has done so much for so many people in our community. Please let me know if I can ever be of help to you in your work with the ABC Charity."

You have done several things in this conversation. You have let him know that you have a good relationship with someone he is close to and respects. You also have given him an acceptable source for the information you have gathered about him. You have paid him a personal compliment and touted the good works of a group or cause he believes in and supports. Lastly, by offering to help, you have not only been supportive of his activities, but you have also indicated to him that you share his feelings for this particular group.

It would be impossible for this prospect to be offended by anything you have done or said in this situation.

VII
Look for common ground.

This may be stating the obvious, but it is important enough to justify placing extra emphasis on the point. Review the material you have gathered with an eye toward anything that will give you something in common with your prospect. Look for individuals who attended the same schools, support the same causes, vote for the same candidates, or any factor that will make the prospect more comfortable with you as an individual and more receptive to you as a salesperson. Virtually everyone will be nicer to someone with whom they have a mutual interest.

One of my goals as a salesperson was to never make a cold call. I have heard about sales managers who demand, and read sales books which recommend constant cold calling on new prospects as a method of keeping one's selling skills sharp. I disagree. This is setting yourself up for failure and disappointment, the two things that in my opinion, should be avoided like the plague.

Let me expand on my suggestion to avoid cold calling. I, obviously, am not suggesting that you avoid contacting new prospects. I am suggesting that you do some background work before you contact a new prospect. Which of these calls do you think has a better chance of success?

Call One: "Hello, Dr. Smith. This is Lee Ledbetter from ABC Corporation. Are you familiar with ABC?"

"Well, actually no".

"Oh, then if I may, let me give you a little background on our company and tell you a little about some of our products."

At this point, you may very well hear something like, "I'm pretty busy right now. Why don't you just send me some literature."

Compare that call to this one.

Call Two: "Hello, Dr. Smith. This is Lee Ledbetter. I am calling at the suggestion of Dr. Jones. He told me that the two of you are very close and often share ideas. He has been using a widget, our new product, and he felt it would be of great benefit to you."

The obvious common ground, in this case, is the relationship with Dr. Jones. But, it doesn't have to be a reference. It can be any fact or set of facts which put the prospect more at ease than in the true cold call described in the first example.

VIII

Read everything you can about the leaders in the industry you are dealing with.

This is a great way to learn your customer's business and it will help you understand what makes someone successful in a particular industry. You will be better informed and better able to share ideas and programs for success with others. Correspond with industry leaders. In most cases they will respond to your letter which will not only give you valuable input, but will provide you with letters you can refer to in dealings with your clients. Again, the object here is to find common ground and avoid making true cold calls at all costs!

IX

Know how your prospects make decisions.

This is a critical aspect of studying people. I have known salespeople who literally spent years calling on a prospect only to learn that the person they were talking to didn't have the authority to make a purchase. This is a question you should ask directly of the person you are calling on. Don't beat around the bush. Don't equivocate. "Mr. Z, are you the person who makes the buying decisions for your organization?"

Even if he says yes, ask him to define the process more specifically. Are others involved in the decision making process? Is there a time frame involved? Must purchases be budgeted? If so, what is the budgetary process? You can create the proper questions to ask depending on the situation. I just want you to understand the necessity of knowing what it will take to turn this prospect into a customer.

I have discussed the specifics of determining how a prospect makes buying decisions. However, you must also understand the subtleties. Some clients will buy from you based on your personal relationship even if your price is slightly higher than your competitors. Others are totally price conscious or concerned about service following the sale. You must know what is most important to that individual.

Even more subtle psychological factors are often at work. Some people cannot make decisions and want you to make decisions for them. They literally want to delegate the decision making to you.

Some clients enjoy the banter over pricing or sale terms and need to feel they have "won" every negotiation. Many prospects rely on gut feeling or emotion in making decisions. Others consider such actions a sign of weakness and pride themselves on only "looking at the facts."

Ask questions. Do research on the prospect. Talk to their staff people. Look at their past history. In short, do whatever is necessary to understand the prospect's decision making process.

Study people. Your life will be more fun and you will enhance your chances for success if you make this process a lifetime quest.

All my love,
Mother

Chapter Six

ORGANIZE, ORGANIZE, ORGANIZE

*"Discipline by others is tyranny; self-discipline
is the only true freedom."*
— MY MOTHER

Dear Son,

Every salesperson I have ever known who has achieved
long-term success has been well organized. You must
learn to organize, organize, organize! I wrote it three
times for emphasis to stress how important organization is if you are to succeed in sales.

The most common lament I heard from low achievers was, "If only I could get organized." I seldom heard

salespeople complain that they didn't understand their product or service. I would on rare occasions hear complaints about their lack of support, their ability to make proper presentations, or their failure to receive the necessary cooperation from their clients. I constantly heard that same statement over and over again, "if only I could get organized." I had little sympathy for this concern and would usually voice my feelings by reminding the complainer that they could get organized by employing a combination of effort and discipline. It is refreshing and encouraging to know that an element so critical to sales success is entirely within your own control. Never admit to yourself that becoming organized is out of your reach. Demand of yourself, mastery of this key ingredient of success. I have seen some individuals achieve short-term success in sales without good organizational skills. However, they either learned these skills, were wise enough to realize their shortcomings and hire someone else to do it for them, or they inevitably fell back to mediocrity. Let me begin with a few, specific suggestions:

1. Have a 'To Do" list every day. Take great care in what you put on this list and once an item is on the list, take even greater care in seeing that you do what is required to be able to check it off the list. I try to end every day by preparing my "To Do" list for the next day. You should never go to work wondering what you are going to do that day. By having a well organized list of specific items, you want to accomplish for the day, you have created short term goals.

This approach will also help the longer term, over-arching goals that I wrote about earlier find their way into your life.

2. Prioritize the items on your "To Do" list This is an important part of the organizational process. Don't just list items and then try to accomplish them in the order you have listed them. Take time and carefully prioritize items in their order of proper importance. I always made the list in whatever order they came to mind. Then I would go back and to the left of the listed item, I would place the priority number. I'd then do everything possible to accomplish the top priority on the list before moving to item two. Then I would move to the second item and proceed accordingly.

3. At the end of each day, summarize what you have done and record the lessons you learned that day in a diary. Go back and read the diary on a regular basis. You will find goals emerging from the pages of that diary. Also, write down any mistakes you feel you may have made as a way of purging them. Write them down. Replay in your mind what you should have done and then forget about your mistake. Try to learn from your mistakes and build on your successes.

4. Make comprehensive notes after each phone call or meeting and keep those notes in a consistent format so that you can retrieve them when necessary. Write down everything you learned from each contact. Once you have evaluated the day's performance and made the appropriate entries, make the "To Do" list for the next day.

(Item #3 refers to overall lessons, Item #4 refers to specific details regarding a particular client such as, what they are buying, their reactions to presentations, etc.)

5. Know when to quit. It is often just as important to know when to quit as it is to know when to persevere. If a prospect is obviously never going to lead to business, and you are quite certain of this fact, then you should strike them from your list and stop wasting your time. There are times when the person you are calling on has a relative who is a competitor or for any one of many reasons you just may not have proper chemistry with that person. You need to recognize that fact, accept it, and be willing to turn the page and move on.

It is important that you never take rejection personally in selling. Remember that you are looking to do business with only a small percentage of the prospects in order to be a tremendous success. You should learn only to count the yeses and learn to ignore the noes. This is a very important part of the organizational process.

6. Always make time for prospecting. No matter what field you may find yourself engaged in, you will start with a large list of prospects and constantly narrow it down to those who will ultimately become your clients. A variety of reasons will cause you to lose clients over time which will have nothing to do with your failure to service the account. People will move or be transferred, they will die, they will be promoted, or their companies will be taken over, or merged out of existence. These are things that you cannot control and you must always be working to fill in the other end of the pipeline.

That is why it is important for you to constantly organize your time in such a way that, while doing everything necessary to service your existing client base, you always allow time for prospecting and the necessary ground work to pave the way for the creation of new relationships. Of course, temper this advice with my earlier suggestion that you do everything possible to avoid making cold calls. Have some common thread, a reference or some way to make the prospecting call an initial contact instead of a cold call.

7. Make time for inspirational materials. No matter how busy or successful you become, allow some time every day for inspirational input by reading motivational materials or attending uplifting meetings. You can get careless in this area, and before you know it, negative thoughts and feelings will begin to creep into your mind. These unwelcome intruders will begin to chip away at even the most determined, positive thinking individual. Practice what makes you a success in the first place. Never forget that we all need constant motivational input.

8. Prepare thoroughly for every phone call or meeting. Even if you are calling only to schedule a meeting, think through the call before you make it. Have a specific purpose for every call or meeting and never lose sight of that objective. There is no place in sales for wasted effort. Never do anything without a purpose. Don't call just to make small talk, unless the purpose of the call is to gather personal information about the client.

9. Do required paperwork on a timely basis. In most sales jobs, you are required to fill out periodic reports to keep supervisors and/or the home office informed as to your activities. I am not a great believer in much of the paperwork required by many sales organizations. However, a certain amount of paperwork is necessary, and whether you agree with what is required or not, internal politics will demand that you conform to whatever requirements are placed upon you. I have been told that the very personality traits that tend to make an exceptional salesperson are not those that insure attention to paperwork details.

Don't accept that kind of thinking. Do whatever you are required to do. It is part of your job. Don't have managers say about you, "Well, he just doesn't take care of the paperwork." Such comments will interfere with your progress and will have an indirect negative impact on your sales activities.

Never procrastinate! Do the required paperwork at

the end of each day if possible. If not, do it at the earliest possible time. There is nothing worse for a salesperson to do than to burden themselves with guilt. If you know you were supposed to do something which you haven't done, you will have that awareness in your mind. It *will* affect your concentration and your ability to do what you need to do.

10. Send regular (preferably weekly) communications to your clients. I referred to this in my first letter as a great way to share feelings and let people know you are thinking of them. But, you must do it in an organized fashion. Try to personalize the mailout whenever possible. However, if you don't have a personal message, send a communication anyway. You will need to read general news, magazines, industry publications, etc. which your client may not have seen, and anything else which might provide material which is of interest to them. Record what you sent to whom and when you sent it so you can refer to what you sent when you speak to the client or prospect. As I said in my earlier letter, this keeps your name in front of them, and it also is another way of having something of interest to discuss with them.

11. Always remember to thank those who help you achieve success. This will not only make the person who helped you along the way feel good, but you will derive a morale boost as well. This too should be done in an organized way to insure that you never forget those who helped you. Keep a list of the communications you send to remind you if too much time has gone by without an appropriate contact. If someone helped you with a referral, or helpful suggestion, you never want them to think of you as ungrateful. You also want them to repeat the act of kindness or support, if asked, in the future. They will be far more likely to do so if you remember to thank them for past actions.

Put those to whom you owe a particular debt of gratitude on a "Thank You List". Drop them a note every time you accomplish something special. Share your joy with them and remind them that you could not have done it without their help and support at a critical time.

12. Follow the goal achievement process set out in my letter on working more on yourself than on your product or service. Remember the four steps:

1 . Write it down.

2. Specify a definite time for accomplishment of the goal.

3. List the reasons why you think the goal will be accomplished.

4. List what you will have to do for the goal to become reality.

Never take this process for granted, no matter how small the goal. You must always continue to be organized in your approach to goal setting and goal achievement.

13. Master the necessary product knowledge and keep yourself current. As I wrote earlier, I believe you should spend more time working on yourself than on your product or service. I also wrote that you must know enough about your product or service to be able to market it successfully. The key to doing both successfully is organization. You have a limited amount of time and you must use that time wisely.

There is great truth to the old cliche, "If you want something done, get a busy man to do it." The reason this statement holds true is because busy people have found it necessary to organize themselves. Most people could at least double their output if they would just organize themselves better. You must have a certain basic knowledge of your product or service. You can't avoid it. Thus, accept it as a challenge and as a duty. Use it as a starting point in planning your schedule. This first step will dictate the rest of your scheduling and ensure an organized allocation of all your available time.

Determine what materials you must read and what meetings you must attend to stay current on your product or service. Then schedule that time and adhere strictly to that schedule. By planning your time carefully, and by doing so as far in advance as possible, you will be able to stay abreast of all necessary information and still have plenty of time to do everything else you need to do in order to succeed.

14. Allow time to understand your client's business. It is not enough to know your product or service, and it is not enough to know yourself. To maximize your potential, you must thoroughly understand your customer's business. This accomplishes several purposes. By knowing more about your customer's business, you create common ground. You are able to talk to clients about what they care most about — their business. Remember, the clients expect and assume you know a lot about your product and service. However, they do not expect or assume you will know very much about their business. When they discover that you do know a lot about their business, they will be pleasantly surprised and will place you in a different category. They will treat you with much greater respect and believe me, they will do more business with you.

You must allocate the time to be sure that you come to understand your client's business. The first step is to learn the vocabulary of a business. I have always said that if I know the vocabulary of a subject, I can sound like an expert. Read industry publications. Much of what you need to learn can be done while waiting to see clients. You should also ask a lot of questions. Most people enjoy talking about their own businesses, especially when they can show off their own knowledge. Never pass up a chance to learn from experts.

Let me make one specific suggestion to you about learning from your clients or prospects. When I first began, I selected one prospect and made a request of him. I promised to never try and sell him anything and to never waste his time if he would just "adopt" me by helping to teach me his business and to be available to answer questions which would help me better serve his colleagues. My adopted mentor not only was kind enough to help, but because of my unique approach, he became one of my best clients. I then went out and asked someone else to "adopt" me. During my career, I asked fourteen different people to adopt me and got only one refusal. Of the remaining thirteen, I eventually did business with eleven of them!

15. Periodically evaluate all time commitments in your life and make adjustments to reflect your true priorities. Many people find themselves overwhelmed by demands on their time. Without realizing it, they will allow their time to be filled with insignificant, trivial commitments which do not contribute to the realization of meaningful goals. All we have in life is our time. Reduced to its most simple terms, life is nothing but the sum total of all our time. How we spend that time determines the quality of our lives. If we allow our schedules to be controlled by others and for our time to be used in the pursuit of things which are not goals or priorities in our lives, then most of our time is wasted and our real goals fail to be realized or even pursued.

16. When a customer complains, always assume they are right. This is not only good advice in customer relations, but also in time management. Customers don't want to waste their time. They very rarely make a complaint without foundation. If you spring to the defense of your company, you not only injure the relationship but waste a lot of time. Listen to the complaint and try to deliver what the customer wants, as soon as possible, and with a minimum of fanfare.

17. Never forget a promise. Some prospects will test you. They will ask for something, get a commitment from you, and then wait to see if you perform as promised. If you forget even the smallest promise, they will conclude that you are undependable and you are unlikely to ever do business with that individual. I tried to create situations where a prospect would ask me to perform a specific task. This would give me an opportunity to demonstrate my dependability. One of my favorite questions was, "Would you like me to follow up on that?" When the prospect said yes, then I had a reason for future communication. When responding in writing, I always began the letter with, "As promised in response to your request, please find the information regarding XYZ." This served as a reminder that a commitment had been fulfilled.

— *from Mother, with Love* —

Follow these suggestions, and you will always be organized. If you are always organized, you will have taken a giant step toward success.

All my love,
Mother

Chapter Seven

LEARN COMMUNICATION SKILLS

"Tell me and I will forget.
Show me and I will remember.
Involve me and I will understand."
— CONFUCIUS

Dear Son,

The most important communication skill you can master is the ability to communicate with yourself. Many people become talented, external communicators and sought after public speakers, but never learn to control the constant internal dialogue which is a part of all of us.

It is helpful to learn good external communication skills. But it is critical that you learn how to communicate effectively with yourself. Each of us has a conscious and a subconscious mind. It is vital to understand the different functions of each and to learn how to coordinate their diverse activities. Napoleon said, *"The strong man is the one who is able to intercept at will the communication between the senses and the mind."*

The conscious mind directs our activities. It allows us to move, to gather information through our senses, to judge and to react to situations. It is how we choose to do one thing rather than another. We, as human beings, don't just act on instinct. We are rational creatures endowed with the divine power to THINK. Through conscious effort, we can decide what we are going to think about. This divine creativity means that we have the power to write our own script and to become what we choose to think, if only we will grasp control of this awesome force.

By comparison, our subconscious mind is the reservoir of all the events and activities which collectively make up our "life". The key characteristic of the subconscious mind is that it blindly accepts everything which we say or do. It doesn't react or judge, it simply accepts what is thrust upon it. This means that the subconscious mind becomes whatever is provided to it by the conscious mind. Consider the simplicity and the power of this process. Our subconscious, as a result of the information it is fed, becomes a reflection of what we truly believe ourselves to be. If we hold a subconscious image of ourselves which is different from the results we are currently getting in the conscious world, then the subconscious will exert its overpowering influence to bring us back into conformity with this internal image. Unfortunately, as a result of negative upbringing and environmental factors, the vast majority of individuals find that their subconscious pulls them backwards, toward mediocre performance rather than spurring them on to greater heights. Those individuals don't know the secret I am about to share with you: THROUGH CONSCIOUS INPUT YOU CAN CHANGE THE BELIEF SYSTEM OF YOUR SUB-CONSCIOUS MIND.

Once you accept the truth of this statement you can literally rewrite your personal history. You can, through repetition, practice and consciously directed effort, change anything you do not like about your subconscious programming. Revel in your creative power as a human being. If you neglect to take advantage of this strength then you will have wasted the greatest legacy you have inherited from all your human predecessors.

Stop often and listen to your internal dialogue. Is it positive? Is it constructive? Is it contributing to your success? Is it moving you toward an important goal? Does it serve a high priority in your life? If the answer to any of these questions is "no" then you need to take better control of this important internal communication. It is amazing what you can learn about yourself if you will just stop and listen. You will come to know what you really believe, what you really think of yourself, and the extent to which those beliefs are a blueprint for success or a formula for certain failure. If you listen carefully and observe your own actions, you will find, in the long run, a striking similarity between the thoughts which you are allowing to dominate your mind and the actions you are taking.

If there is a substantial difference between your thoughts and your actions then one or the other will have to change. You will either have to move your thoughts toward conformity with your actions or you can be certain that your actions, over the long run, will begin to conform with your thoughts. By listening to yourself carefully, and the practice of controlling what you hear, you will discover a great truth — you can control those thoughts and by doing so change your actions and the direction of your life.

Most people spend more time listening to what other people say to them and about them than what they are saying to themselves about themselves. Master your internal communications and you can change anything about yourself. W. Clement Stone tells us that, *"Self suggestion makes you master of yourself."* You can reprogram your basic belief system, choosing to evict those thoughts which limit you and to replace them with thoughts which empower you. You can decide not to think about bad things. You can consciously think about constructive, positive things.

You can also learn to eliminate worry, one of the most non-productive activities known to man. Worrying about something does nothing positive. Replace "worry time" with constructive thoughts. Concentrate on the result you want to achieve and free your subconscious mind to direct you in the proper manner. Success is the natural state, and the one toward which our subconscious will move us if we will just get out of our own way.

The possibilities are unlimited. You can, within the realm of reality, be anything you want to be. If you can totally convince your subconscious that something is true, then it becomes true in so far as it impacts on your life.

Napoleon Hill understood the strength which comes from mastering your internal dialogue: "You are searching for the magic key that will unlock the door to the source of power; and yet, you have the key in your own hands and you may make use of it the moment you learn to control your thoughts."

You can overcome the negative input of past events, setbacks, disappointments, or destructive thought patterns. Like so many things, just wishing won't make it happen. The key word again is practice. You must start by listening and watching your actions. Then select simple phrases to substitute for any thoughts you find are nonproductive and lead to undesirable actions.

For instance, if you hear yourself thinking negative thoughts, begin to repeat over and over to yourself, "I am in charge of my own thoughts." Practice substituting this instructional statement in place of the negative thoughts you want to eliminate. Then add positive, constructive thoughts in place of the earlier negative input. It won't be easy at first, but with time and constant practice, you will get better at it.

As you begin to see results, you will realize the power inherent in controlling your own internal dialogue. You will begin to get excited and each success will encourage you to practice harder and to be ever more diligent in mastering this process. In time you will be able to move beyond eliminating the negative and begin to program constructive thoughts into your continuing dialogue. Remember the steps:

1. Listen.

2. See how closely your actions mirror your thoughts.

3. Decide how you want to reprogram your thinking.

4. Begin by eliminating the negative and inserting a reminder that you are in control.

5. Add the constructive thoughts that you want to control your future actions.

6. Practice.

You cannot communicate well if you do not listen well. You communicate sincerity by asking the right questions and expressing legitimate concern, but you destroy the impression if you don't show rapt attention to the answer. The same is true if you don't listen carefully to a question asked of you. There is nothing worse than responding incorrectly to a request which demonstrates that you really did not hear the question.

The most important sentence you should master is, "I don't know." Don't ever guess if you aren't sure. There is no shame in admitting you don't know the answer to a question. By agreeing to get the answer and calling back, you have a reason for the prospect to accept your call in the future. While I don't recommend it as a general practice, I have said, "I don't know" even when I knew the answer because I felt it would improve my chances of getting a future audience with the prospect. Most clients will be impressed by your honesty in admitting you don't know the answer to a particular question. They will almost always be courteous enough and curious enough to take your call when you come back to them with the answer.

Listen to the prospect and respond directly. Don't be evasive in your words or actions. Take notes. Make it obvious that you feel what is being said to you is important and worthy of being written down. Let the prospect know that you are writing down what they are saying because you think it is important and you want to be able to recall every detail correctly.

~ from Mother, with Love ~

It is sometimes more important to hear what your prospect is saying than to have them listen to what you are saying. Lyndon Johnson reportedly had a sign on his desk that read, *"If you're talking then you ain't learning."* Kahil Gibran, author of <u>The Prophet</u> wrote, *"I've learned silence from the talkative."* Many people spend time learning how to be a good speaker but never learn to be a good listener. Don't neglect the passive part of being a good communicator. Learn to listen. It is also important that you go beyond hearing the words. You must be able to decipher what the prospect really means. I referred to that concept earlier in the letter suggesting that you study people.

Harry Truman was a good listener. He could detect what people really meant. He wrote, *"Whenever a fellow tells me he is bipartisan, I know he is going to vote against me."* Practice listening. It is a great art to master.

As to what you say in direct presentations, practice is the best teacher. You can make your presentations in the shower, while driving, or anytime you are alone. Even when you are in a crowd, you can rehearse a presentation in your mind. Remember to make the best possible use of your constant stream of thoughts. There is no need to let this valuable time go to waste. Control these thoughts and make them constructive. Practicing a particular presentation is one of the best uses of this time.

I always tried to say everything that was necessary to be said in the fewest possible words. I always tried to ask as many questions as possible without appearing stilted or contrived. It isn't enough for you to know the truth of what you are saying. Emerson said, *"Eloquence is the power to translate a truth into a language perfectly intelligible to the person to whom you speak."* Stop often and ask questions. Make the prospect a participant in the process. As Confucius advised, by involving the listener, you move them closer to understanding.

A salesman can't just say words and be effective. It is a salesman's job to persuade the listener. Imagine that you know everything there is to know about your product or service but cannot persuasively communicate to your prospect. You have accomplished nothing. Your job as a salesman is to sell something. You must persuade someone to say "yes." They must accept your argument that they need your product or service, otherwise, you have not succeeded in your mission as a salesman.

There are several keys to making a persuasive presentation. Don't speak in a monotone. Vary your tone, your inflection, and your volume. Pause periodically. I found it better to pause in the middle of a thought rather than at the end of a thought. This made it easier to retain the listener's attention.

Always try to be different in the way you make your presentations. One of my future letters will be devoted to the importance of being different. Be creative. Use your imagination. There is nothing worse for a salesman than to become the worst four letter word in the English language — a BORE!

Smile a lot. Laugh as much as is appropriate. Find ways to inject humor into your presentation.

Direct communication is important and it is in the one-on-one situations that listening is at least as important as what you say. However, public speaking is another aspect of being a good communicator. It is extremely important that you learn to be a good public speaker. Most people are terrified to speak in public. When you do it, and do it well, you exude confidence and power, and make people want to do business with you. Some people think that good public speakers are born. Some are, but most are not. I am convinced that almost anyone can become an acceptable public speaker. The key traits of a good public speaker are:

1. Enthusiasm for the subject matter. It is difficult to convey excitement where none exists. If you aren't enthusiastic about the subject, then don't accept the invitation to speak. I have heard many poor speakers convey enthusiasm about their subject and, therefore, make a successful presentation. I have also seen good speakers fail by appearing glib and uninvolved with their subject matter.

2. Use of humor if relevant to the subject matter. Nothing is more annoying than a speaker telling a funny story which is irrelevant to the subject matter. It comes off as contrived and insincere. However, humor, used properly, is a hallmark of good public speaking. Humor puts the audience at ease. It beckons them to come along with you on an interesting journey.

George Bernard Shaw wrote, *"My method is to take the utmost trouble to find the right thing to say, and then to say it with the utmost levity."* What great advice! No matter how serious your subject, it will be better received if sprinkled with a fine helping of humor.

3. Avoidance of any use of notes except when presenting highly technical information. Listeners are always impressed by a speaker who can speak freely on their subject matter without reading or constantly referring to notes. Mrs. Ghandi was once asked how her husband could speak at great length without ever referring to a note. She replied that, "Most people think one thing, say another, and do yet a third. On the other hand, for Ghandi, they are all one and the same." This is an extremely valid and valuable lesson. This is why it is very difficult to sell a product or service you don't believe in. It is difficult to convince an audience that you hold a deep conviction about a subject if you have your head down and are reading a script.

It is also difficult to appear enthusiastic when reading a speech. It is easy to become boring, the worst of all possible words to apply to a speaker. If you must use notes, then use a blackboard and write the material up in advance of your presentation, or use an overhead projector. Either approach will allow you to refer to supporting material but not be so obvious about it that it distracts or bores your audience.

4. Mastery of the material being presented. Most people can discuss their area of special interest in almost any forum simply because they know so much about it. When one attempts to speak on a subject without adequate knowledge, you can expect a poor, weak performance which is not persuasive.

5. Use of visual aids. My experience both as a speaker and as a member of the audience has convinced me that the proper use of props or visual aids can greatly enhance a presentation. Again, like humor, the visual aid must fit properly into the overall presentation. Trial lawyers have demonstrated repeatedly that jurors respond favorably to the use of visual aids. Whenever you are preparing a presentation, ask yourself what kind of visual aid would help enhance your presentation. Be creative. Try to make the audience remember you and what you had to say.

The best visual aid I ever used was one of my customers. I had been asked to make a presentation to a group of doctors on one of my company's new products. I thought it would be fun to try something different. I wore a powdered wig and portrayed a British barrister. I asked one of my doctor clients who had used the product with good results to play the role of witness in my little play. I knew he was a bit of a ham, and he gladly accepted. I seated him in front of the room and swore him in as Dr. Mercy from Merciful, Kansas, just as though he were a witness in a trial. I then asked him a series of questions which we had gone over carefully in advance. His testimony was a ringing endorsement of the product. My questions and his answers were filled with humor designed to entertain as well as to inform. The event was a great success. Everyone had a lot of fun, learned important information, and use of our product increased dramatically.

6. Constant practice. Practice in front of a mirror. Check out your facial expressions, your hand gestures, and the movements of your body. Do you move too much? or too quickly? Does this movement detract from your message? I have heard speakers and been so distracted by their movements that I began to watch and anticipate the gestures or movements they were going to make next, instead of concentrating on what they were going to say. Practice will reveal and help you avoid these mistakes.

It is also important to have a "practice" audience. Ask a neighbor, a friend, a fellow employee, or a customer with whom you have an excellent relationship to critique your presentation. For this to be effective, it must be someone who will be honest with you and not just tell you what they think you want to hear.

Being a good communicator also demands that you write well. You can make an outstanding presentation and then destroy everything you have accomplished by sending out a poorly written follow-up letter. Good business letters should be brief and to the point. I always tried to have some kind of personal reference in most business letters. This was part of my never ending attempt to create a personal relationship which would enhance my business relationship. However, any attempt at injecting personal material, other than greetings and well wishes, like humor in a speech, should be relevant to the business purpose of the letter. Otherwise, you should send separate letters.

Never send out a letter with a misspelled word. It is impossible to convey to a prospect that you would be attentive to their needs if you are so careless as to send out a letter which contains either spelling or punctuation errors. This is extremely unprofessional and conveys an image of carelessness.

Take great joy in the process of becoming a good communicator. Being a good communicator will be a source of high self-esteem, and a vital factor in personal happiness and success. One who listens closely, speaks persuasively, presents ideas in an entertaining manner, and writes with clarity, is virtually assured of a successful career in sales.

All my love,
Mother

Chapter Eight

DEVELOP A STRONG FEELING OF CONFIDENCE

"Nobody can make you feel inferior without your consent."

— ELEANOR ROOSEVELT

Dear Son,

The feeling of confidence is not an inherited characteristic. You must work hard to develop inner confidence and even harder to maintain that feeling. The process never ends.

Even if you are one of the most successful individuals in the world, you will face much more rejection than acceptance. For that reason, you must have a strong sense of who you are and a calm inner confidence in that self. It is impossible to find success in every presentation. After you develop clients, you will lose them for reasons beyond your control. You must never allow these temporary setbacks to shake your inner confidence.

Learn to run, with the greatest possible speed, away from negative thoughts and feelings about yourself. When others do or say things which would intrude on your feelings of self-confidence, learn to ignore them. I am not suggesting that you avoid learning from your mistakes, or that you should be unwilling to take constructive criticism. I am suggesting you learn that what you do, whether right or wrong, is not who you are. When someone criticizes something you have done, you should not allow your subconscious mind to accept these criticisms as deficiencies in your true self. You are what you are, not what you do. You are what you know yourself to be, not what others perceive you to be.

True self-confidence is the feeling that you are in charge of your own life and can direct it. To turn your life over to others and allow them to direct you is to invite disaster. This can happen without you even realizing it. It is insufficient to say that you will not allow others to run your life. Many people make this assertion, but then spend their entire lives trying to achieve goals which other people set for them. This is not achieving the kind of self-confidence that I am suggesting to you. Such confidence can only be achieved by developing a strong inner feeling of who you are, not by conforming to other people's ideas of what you should be.

The kind of self-confidence which will see you through tough times and disappointments goes beyond positive thinking. It is having an unshakable conviction of who and what you are and accepting that reality. I am sure you know individuals who made a fortune, lost it, and in a few years, made another fortune. Those individuals are able to rebound because of the inner picture they have of themselves. They expect success and it finds them. When they fail, usually in the course of taking a risk to achieve an even greater degree of success, they accept the failure as temporary and proceed. You will know you have arrived at a state of true self confidence when you expect and anticipate success without really thinking about it.

The other end of the spectrum is also true. Those individuals with low self-esteem may find temporary success, but their image of themselves will almost invariably pull them back into failure or mediocrity. Most people lack confidence because they were trained from early childhood with negatives. They were put down by others instead of being built up. They were taught "no" rather than "yes," by "don't" rather than "do." A negative belief will stifle accomplishment. If an objective is made impossible by a limiting belief you must change that belief into a positive force. Everything which is created is preceded by the idea of that thing in someone's imagination. Thomas Carlyle expressed the same thought eloquently:

"The city with all its houses, palaces, steam engines, cathedrals, and huge immeasurable traffic and tumult, what is it but thought, but millions of thoughts made into one — a huge immeasurable Spirit of Thought embodied in brick, in iron, in smoke, dust, palaces, parliaments, coaches, docks, and the rest of it! Not a brick was made but someone had to think of the making of that brick."

The same relationship which exists between ideas and things, exists between confidence and accomplishment. Confidence must precede accomplishment. Henry Ford said, *"If you think you can or think you can't, you're right."* However, confidence and success remain intertwined throughout your life. Confidence can be fragile, and once developed, it must be nurtured. While confidence must precede initial success, once some success has been achieved, that very success becomes an additional building block of confidence. The more success, the more confidence. Likewise, the more confidence, the more success one has.

Once you know yourself, you are free to be that person. You no longer are a slave to becoming what others would have you be. As Napoleon Hill wrote, *"If you do not conquer self, you will be conquered by self."* If your self-confidence depends on what others think of you then you will never really be self-confident or free. You will have only temporary periods during which you match up to someone else's expectations. W. Clement Stone, one of my favorite sources of inspirational material wrote, *"Bondage is ... subjection to external influences and internal negative thoughts and attitudes."*

This same process of getting to know yourself works in developing relationships with others. If you can get an individual to open up to you sufficiently for you to know who they really are, then you can help them better realize their own identity. When you do this, you will have the basis of a close relationship.

Developing the internal communication skills I discussed in my last letter is the essence of creating a strong feeling of self-confidence. When you think about something, it tends to happen. That is why it is critical to think about what you want instead of what you want to avoid. Your subconscious mind doesn't know whether you are thinking about something because you want it to happen or because you want to avoid it. Your subconscious mind only knows that the thought is present and that it wants to move toward those things you think about. Therefore, you must control your thoughts and use them as a vehicle to build the confidence necessary to reach your objectives. In addition to mastering appropriate internal communication skills, my experience convinced me that there were six other keys to developing and maintaining the necessary degree of self-confidence:

~ from Mother, with Love ~

1. Preparation. The knowledge that you are prepared for the task at hand is a vital step towards developing a strong feeling of confidence. Old fashioned hard work is the key to being prepared. The process of doing several of the things I recommended in my earlier letters will help you be prepared.

I recommended that you share love and your feelings of love. The act of sharing love will allow you to develop relationships. If you are in business, then laying the groundwork for people to take your calls, listen to your proposals, and, in general, to be receptive to you is a major step in the process of being prepared. You can prepare for a particular call or event of any kind by reducing stress through proper breathing as described in my second letter.

In my third letter, I wrote to you about learning more about yourself. The process of knowing your personal goals and priorities and understanding what you have to do to make them realities will reduce wasted effort and help you concentrate on what is most important in order to accomplish your objectives. Alexander Graham Bell, the inventor of the telephone, wisely advised that one should, *"Concentrate all your thoughts upon the work at hand."*

Next, I wrote to you about the importance and the challenge of studying people. If you have all the information about a prospect on the PIP sheet then you know how best to approach that individual. By reviewing the sheet before any contact you are always prepared to maximize a particular presentation.

If you organize, organize, organize, then by definition, you will be prepared and with that preparation, will come the confidence needed to succeed.

Mastering external communication skills will allow you to get excited about the prospect of demonstrating those skills. As you practice becoming a more skilled communicator you will look forward, with great anticipation, to the opportunity to use those skills. That excitement will generate confidence.

Each undertaking requires a different type of preparation. In order to be properly prepared, you must fully understand the job at hand and know exactly what preparation is required. You must learn to evaluate each task quickly, but accurately. That is part of the hard work necessary to be fully prepared. Most people take simple things and make them complicated. It is a basic truth that if you are thoroughly prepared, you will be confident in your ability to perform. Don't be intimidated by the magnitude of an undertaking. Every problem, no matter how complicated can be made easier to solve if broken down into a series of small tasks. To quote Henry Ford again, *"Nothing is particularly hard if you divide it into small jobs."*

By breaking a large, complex task down into a series of small, easy to accomplish objectives, you make your job of properly preparing much easier. Total preparation results in confidence. And you can control preparation by simple, hard work. When feelings of inadequacy begin to creep into your consciousness you can often, for a specific undertaking, beat those feelings into submission with thorough preparation.

2. Love yourself. My sales manager told me early in my sales career, *"If you don't toot your own horn, nobody will toot it for you."* I took that advice as a cornerstone in building a successful career. There were bound to be times when others would lose faith and confidence in me. During those times, I had to be sure that I never lost faith in myself.

As the first woman in my field, I felt pressure to succeed not just for myself, but for those who might come after me. I constantly sought the support of other women who had succeeded, especially those who had been pioneers in their fields.

Lucille Ball, a pioneer in television comedy, confirmed my feeling that it was acceptable to love myself. She wrote, *"Love yourself first and everything else falls into line."* There is nothing wrong with going beyond believing in yourself and truly loving yourself. Many people lay the groundwork for their own failure in the name of modesty. Don't fall into this trap. Love yourself first and foremost. This will free you to care and do for others because you won't have to constantly feed your ego to keep it satisfied and quiet.

In my first letter I suggested that you learn to share feelings of love, and that it was important that you actively demonstrate those feelings. The same process should be followed in loving yourself. Don't just mouth the words to yourself, but act like you love yourself and show it. I developed a number of specific ways to be good to myself. First, I would reward myself for the accomplishment of a particular goal or task. I would promise to buy myself a new book or dress I had been eyeing in a shop window as soon as I topped my dollar volume goal for the month. It was important that I always kept my promise to myself. Immediately upon reaching my objective, I purchased my well deserved reward. This became an intriguing game which I could play continuously with myself. It brought the benefits of goals into more immediate focus. It allowed me to enjoy the fruits of my labors in the short term.

Next, I would take real breaks. I would occasionally walk away from all the pressures of my job and my other responsibilities. I would take an entire day to read books I had been wanting to read, or to go to movies I had been hoping to see. I would occasionally go to one of the local museums and lose myself in history or in the artistic productions of others. At other times, I would window shop aimlessly, stopping for lunch with a newspaper or magazine as my only companion.

I always knew when it was time to recharge my batteries. I had an internal clock which went off blaring to me, "Enough is enough." I would, after a day, or in some instances even a half day break, come back refreshed and energized and would be better prepared to reach for higher goals. I was fortunate in that my sales manager understood the need for what he called "quiet time." He wasn't concerned about the quantity of my effort as much as the quality of my results. He knew that a break would allow me to come back with renewed vigor and that my performance would reflect the benefits of my brief respite.

The third thing I did was to compliment myself often and with great enthusiasm. After a particularly gratifying call, I would praise myself in glowing terms as I drove to my next appointment: "Good job, Lee! You were just terrific. I was particularly proud of how you handled the objection and the brief history of the new product. I loved the expression on Dr. Smith's face. He knew the product would help his patients. He came right out and said so and committed to writing regular prescriptions for the product. What a great job you did!"

This kind of praise did two things. It made me feel good immediately, but it also had a longer term impact. This constant barrage of positive input from my conscious mind to my subconscious made me more likely to repeat successful outcomes. I didn't just say that I loved myself. I went further. I showed myself how I felt, and I bought presents for myself. I took real breaks and I bombarded myself with effusive praise.

3. Have your own cheering section made up of people who believe in you. Most of what you need to develop and maintain confidence comes from within. However, even the most confident souls will need outside support at times. It is not a sign of weakness to admit you need help. It is a sign of stubbornness and stupidity to know you need help and not ask for it. The kind of help you need will depend on the time and the place.

Robert Louis Stevenson once said, *"A friend is a gift you give yourself."* How true! I wrote to you earlier about my practice of asking prospective clients to "adopt" me. That practice worked for me. But in asking prospects to adopt me, I was primarily looking for support in learning more about their business and in finding unique ways to approach my clients.

In this letter I am writing about finding support for the more personal side of yourself. If you lose confidence and self-esteem, you are destined to fail. You must find ways to prop up the vital feeling of self-confidence and having your own cheering section is one of the most effective ways of doing this.

I was fortunate that my sales manager was a rare individual. He supervised my sales activities, enforced company rules, provided technical information, offered motivation, and conducted continuous training. In addition, he devoted much of both his work time and his personal time to ensure that his sales representatives developed confidence and self-esteem to maximize their potential. He was there for each of his representatives as a cheering section. No topic was off limits. Most sales managers would restrict their activities to what directly related to sales of the company's products or services. My sales manager believed strongly that we could maximize our potential as salespeople only if we worked to maximize our potential as human beings. He knew that developing confidence was a vital part of our human development. Consequently, he felt that helping us do so was one of the most important things he could do to help us become better salespeople.

Most people are not fortunate enough to have a manager who can double as part of their cheering section. If you fall into that category, you will need to conduct an intensive, all-out search to find the person or persons to make up your own cheering section. It may be a good friend, a relative, a minister, a fellow employee, or even a professional counselor.

To be effective, there are certain conditions which must be met. The members of your cheering section must believe in you totally and unconditionally. They must understand that what you are and what you do are not the same thing. You must be able to share your goals and your priorities with them and have them understand the difference. They must fully appreciate how important a role they play in your life, present and future. They should share in the joy of your accomplishments and be able to understand your frustrations and your disappointments. They should be willing to accept the great responsibility you have entrusted to them. They should know what makes you laugh and what makes you cry. They should love you and know that you love them. They must be thoroughly honest and willing to offer constructive criticism when necessary.

It is critical to accept constructive criticism from someone who believes in you as a guideline for growth and not take the input as a negative put-down. You may well find that you need more than one person who can be supportive of your efforts in different areas of your life. To maximize the help which you can derive from this support system, you must also be thoroughly open and honest with them, both when providing input to them and when making clear what you expect of them. Most people will be highly complimented that you asked them to play such an important role in your life. They will take the task seriously and be an important underpinning for you in those times when you need more support than you are able to generate internally.

4. Creation of an inner retreat where you can replenish your energy and invigorate your soul.
Find an inner retreat. This is a place where you can go in your mind when you must find relief from the stress and strain of daily living. It can be a real place drawn from your memory such as a beach, a lake, or an open field, or it can be a creation of your imagination. It may

change as a new experience or a new thought provides you with vivid images. Practice using different images drawn from your experience or your imagination. You will know when you have found the right image for yourself because of the contentment and sense of satisfaction you will derive from transporting yourself to this inner retreat.

This is another time when the breathing I wrote about to you earlier becomes important. Take one deep breath, close your eyes, and feel yourself begin to relax. Take a second deep breath and feel yourself being transported to your inner retreat. On the third exhalation, feel yourself relax fully and arrive at your inner retreat. Look around and notice every detail of this place which provides you with peace, with strength, and with confidence. This place will be a refuge for you. No one can take it away from you, and it does not require a ticket or travel to get there.

My inner retreat is still a very important part of my life and is something I have never shared with anyone else prior to this letter. My inner retreat has been a private chapel. During my sales career it was a place I could always go to restore my confidence any time it had been shaken. Initially, this was not something I could do well. It took great practice, but in time, I got better. I finally reached a point where no matter how bad an experience I had, or how depressing an event might be, I could flee to my inner retreat and overcome the negative impact of whatever had occurred. One of the great secrets of my success in selling was my ability to flee to my inner retreat.

People might think you quite strange if you talk much about your inner retreat! But, I predict in years to come, the experts will begin to openly teach the need for accessing an inner retreat. I do think you should keep this process private. Make it something you rely on and turn to whenever the need arises. I kept my retreat a secret until now not because of what people would think, but because I wanted one place in the world which was truly mine. To share the details of my inner retreat would, in my case, have destroyed its effectiveness as a place where I could find peace and contentment.

In some ways it is like allowing yourself to be a child again. Children use their imaginations to create worlds which only they are privy to. The same process can be used by adults, but it is a sad legacy of our society that few adults avail themselves of this opportunity. The great artist, Pablo Picasso, once wrote, *"When I was a kid I drew like Michelangelo. It took me years to draw like a kid."* He only became successful when he retreated into his own imagination and allowed the child inside himself to emerge.

Let me get to the details of my inner retreat. I practiced with several possibilities before arriving at what was the best retreat for me. This doesn't mean that you should accept my creation and adopt it as your own. I recommend strongly that you experiment, as I did, in developing what works best for you. This should be an intensely personal creation. It is your creation. Its sole purpose is to enrich your life. Some people would do better drawing on an actual experience which they have had at the beach, on a mountain top, or in a totally restful setting. Maybe due to my limited experience and less than idyllic childhood, it was difficult for me to draw on personal experience in creating the proper kind of inner retreat. Therefore, I had to resort to my imagination.

I always loved green plants, trees, and colorful flowers. Therefore, I built a garden for myself which contained all types of plants, towering trees, and the most beautiful flowers imaginable. They were of every color and every type. Some grew along the ground, others dangled from the tree tops, and others clung to the wall like colorful ivy. Through the garden ran a babbling brook which went in and out of huge boulders, some of which were covered with soft moss while others glistened from the sunlight which broke through cracks within the thick foliage. It was possible for me to sit on several of the rocks and feel the cool texture of the rock beneath my skin. There were also open areas where I could stroll and feel the warmth of the sun. The small furry animals which populated my retreat were enormously friendly, and whenever I came into the garden, they would flock to sit in my lap or rub their furry bodies against my legs. Remember, this was my garden; I built it. It was a product of my imagination and, therefore, it could contain whatever I wanted it to contain. I wasn't limited by the laws of nature, only by my imagination.

There were other special features about this inner retreat. For one thing, I was much larger than in real life. I not only felt big and powerful, but in fact was big and powerful. I could take animals and hold them in my hands. I could walk across a large expanse of this garden with a few giant strides. I am sure by now you can already realize the advantages which this garden brought to me. It was quiet; it was peaceful; it was reassuring; it was the ultimate. Imagine how powerful I could be within this kingdom I created for myself. The animals did my bidding. The water in the brook would change temperature as I commanded. The wind would blow, the sun would shine. It would even rain on my personal command. How could one exposed to that kind of power and control over nature itself not come away with a feeling of confidence and power. After much practice, I found that by closing my eyes and taking a few short breaths as I described earlier, I could transport myself to this magical kingdom. A few minutes within the confines of my beautiful garden, and I would be revived and ready to tackle any obstacle. By creating a place where I could be totally confident, my mind had a place to go to be invigorated and refreshed.

I stress to you that it is very important that you create your own private inner retreat. Remember, you are not bound by reality, you are bound only by your imagination, and whenever you feel weak or ineffective or question your own talents or abilities, flee with all due haste to your inner retreat where you can make the rules.

5. Accept tough challenges and never take the easy way out. General George S. Patton urged his troops, *"Accept the challenges so that you may feel the exhilaration of victory."* If you accept the easy route you will never maximize your growth potential. When you tackle tough jobs and handle them successfully, you get wonderful fuel for your confidence.

Never use fear as an excuse for refusing to try. Write this short poem by Edgar Guest on a small card and carry it with you. Read it whenever you feel fear creeping into your awareness:

What is the thought that is in your mind?
Is fear running through it?
If so, tackle the next you find,
by thinking you're going to do it.

Concentrate on your goals. Think about what you want, not what you want to avoid. The greatest way to overcome fear is to do that which you fear the most. Anything you are afraid of controls you. If you avoid a situation or an opportunity out of fear you have become a slave to that fear and you must overcome it. Ask yourself, what is the worst that can happen? Examine the fear. Investigate it. Truth will reveal most fears to be ungrounded. Then proceed.

Do it. There is nothing which will do more to build confidence than to attack a fear head on and conquer it. Don't anticipate instant victories. Fear is a persistent force. It can only be overcome with greater persistence. Eleanor Roosevelt understood dealing with fear as well as her husband did. She wrote, *"I believe that anyone can conquer fear by doing the things he fears to do, provided he keeps doing them until he gets a record of successful experiences behind him."* Once you know the worst that can happen and do it anyway you will find that you survived because you attacked the fear rather than gave into it. You are now a stronger and better person for it.

One of the best ways I found to attack a specific fear was to take a moment and count my blessings. I was always able to find someone with a bigger problem than mine. A sales representative from another district of our company used to say often, "I cried because I had no shoes until I saw the man who had no feet." That statement always served to put a problem in perspective for me and helped me to confront a fear rather than give into it.

I was a much stronger person after overcoming a life threatening illness. When the doctor tells you that you have cancer, you have no choice but to confront your fear. Based on my experience, you can't really live until you are unafraid to die. Once you confront and conquer your fear of death, you are free to live. You also can put all other fears into proper perspective.

~ from Mother, with Love ~

Some people feel that you can't fail if you don't have a destination. That is often why those kinds of people refuse to set a goal. If they don't try then they can't fail. They can always say, "I could do it if I really wanted to." This excuse makes it acceptable for them to fail. They will never know the exhilaration of accomplishment. I would rather fail mightily trying to achieve great things than to squander my life away trying to avoid the pain that comes with disappointment. I believe that in business, as in life, it is better to have loved and lost than never to have loved at all!

You do not build an effective memory bank of accomplishment by taking on only the easiest of tasks. I agree with Booker T. Washington when he wrote, *"I have learned that success is to be measured not so much by the position that one has reached in life as by the obstacles which he has overcome while trying to succeed."*

You know if you are always opting for the easy route. Challenge yourself. Accept tough assignments. Remember Thomas Paine's words, *"The harder the conflict, the more glorious the triumph."* Revel in your victories. And even when temporary failures arise, know in your heart that you believed enough in yourself to accept the tough assignment. That knowledge alone will contribute to your sense of well being and add to your feeling of confidence.

6. Read biographies of people who have accomplished great things. Their stories will inspire you. You will also be motivated by the fact that many of them rose from humble beginnings to reach greatness. In my next letter, I will give you more reasons to immerse yourself in the life stories of great achievers.

7. Take each task you do seriously but don't take yourself too seriously. Approach each task with enthusiasm and excitement. Take every opportunity to learn and to grow. Do not accept any task as a test of your self worth. True self-esteem will allow you to approach any task with humor. Know you can't fail; you can only progress either by successfully completing the task or by learning from the experience.

Thomas Edison, reflecting on his career, said, *"I never did a day's work in my life. It was all fun."* What a great way to be able to look back on one's life. Edison took his work very seriously, but he approached it with a good-natured attitude. He viewed himself as blessed to have the good fortune to spend his days having fun. We can all emulate his approach. I can honestly say that my career in sales has been enormously satisfying, not just because of the sales I've made or the money I've earned, but because of the fun I have had. Every day presented exciting opportunities to meet new people, to strengthen old relationships and to exchange ideas.

— from Mother, with Love —

I learned to look at each day as an opportunity to enjoy myself and to have fun. This approach enabled me to take my responsibilities seriously but to avoid taking myself too seriously.

Remember the goal should always be to expect and anticipate success. You should also remember that confidence can be fragile and must always be worked on and kept strong. You must be diligent to do everything possible to keep your self-confidence high. Without it, you cannot be a long-term success. Keep yourself inspired. Guard against negative intruders. Believe in yourself so strongly that failure or defeat are only temporary side trips on the shining path to success.

All my love,
Mother

Chapter Nine

NEVER GIVE UP

"It is not the critic who counts, not the man who points out how the strong man stumbled, or where the doer of deeds could have done them better. The credit belongs to the man who is actually in the arena; whose face is marred by dust and sweat and blood; who strives valiantly; who errs and comes short again and again; who knows the great enthusiasm of great devotion; who spends himself in a worthy cause; who at best, knows in the end, the triumph of high achievement, and who at the worst if he fails, at least fails while daring greatly."

— THEODORE ROOSEVELT

Dear Son,

Life is not a short term contest. It is a long series of challenging events. In the letter on organization, I told you to make an ongoing effort to record your experiences. If experiences are unpleasant, learn what mistakes you made and how similar mistakes can be avoided in the future. Then, and this is most important, turn the page on that mistake and go on. Do not dwell on past errors. Simply learn from them and proceed. However, do dwell on your successes and accomplishments. Play these over and over in your mind. Experience the feelings you had at the time you achieved success.

When a goal is accomplished, set a new goal. Goal setting is an unending process. Never think you have "arrived." Always keep creating new and distant targets for yourself. You should also never give up out of futility and throw up your hands and quit. This is not an option for a human being.

Periodically, take stock of what you are doing and don't be afraid to change. I was once told that no one is more ignorant than the person who continues to pursue the same course of action but expects to achieve a different result. Welcome change as growth. If you know where you want to go and what you are doing isn't getting you there, have the courage to change your route while keeping your eye focused on the ultimate destination. Be willing to experiment.

Learn to accept what life gives you and go on. This is an extremely important concept and I will repeat it in bold letters:

LEARN TO ACCEPT
WHAT LIFE GIVES YOU AND GO ON.

Now let me explain the meaning of this statement. I am not suggesting that you passively accept what life gives you. Virtually every part of every letter I have written to you so far has been aimed at teaching you how to affect your life in a positive manner. However, there will be times when goals will appear distant, when failures will mount, and difficulties will arise. In many ways, this is when you will truly be tested as a human being. If every task you undertook worked immediately, you would grow bored with the lack of challenges. You must learn to experience the trip and enjoy the voyage as well as to exult when you reach the destination.

When you meet with a temporary defeat, analyze it, accept responsibility for it, make any necessary adjustments and have the fortitude to proceed. I have known people who have worked very hard toward a particular goal. Then an event in their life occurs, whether it is a divorce, death of a loved one, a business reversal, or any one of a number of events. At that point, they throw up their hands and decide that life is against them, and give up completely or accept mediocrity as their lot in life. Never, ever, accept a single event or unpleasant occurrence as anything more than a temporary setback which should be experienced, learned from, and moved away from.

The earliest golf balls had smooth covers. Then it was discovered that after a ball had been roughed up it would go farther. That is the reason that modern golf balls are manufactured with dimpled covers. So it is with life. It takes some rough spots in your life to make you go your farthest.

Nobody enjoys a complainer. Whatever hand life has dealt you, play it out. Assume responsibility for what happens to you. This is an extremely important concept for you to grasp. I have known people who have gone into business with a partner and had it fail to work out. The partner either proved to be incompetent, or in some cases, outright dishonest. In one instance, the assets of a business were stolen by one of the partners who left town and was never heard from again. One could handle that type of situation with wringing hands and gnashing teeth while cursing the fates that created the situation. It could also be handled far better by assuming responsibility for having selected that particular partner and accepting the results of that partnership. Having learned from the experience, one can move on to avoid repeating that mistake in the future.

When I wrote to you about developing confidence, one of the suggestions I made was that you read biographies of great people. I made that suggestion not just because I felt you would be inspired by their successes, but because I felt you would be encouraged by their persistence. I now repeat that suggestion as the first step in a three pronged program for dealing with frustration and developing a keen sense of persistence.

1. **Read the biographies of great people.**

2. **Build a library of inspirational materials and use them throughout the day, every day.**

3. **Recall successful past experiences.**

Let us now examine each of the three steps in this program for positive persistence.

1. Read the biographies of great people. The history books are replete with people who succeeded because they persisted and did not give up. Thomas Edison is often cited as such an example. He would work on an invention for years, incurring failure after failure after failure. He never counted the lack of success as a failure. He looked upon each experiment as eliminating one possibility for accomplishing his goal. Eventually, he would eliminate thousands and arrive, as in the case of the electric light, with the one method that worked. I am certain that Thomas Edison did not sit around his laboratory wringing his hands over failures. He shared his feelings about the pursuit of success when he wrote *"Many of life's failures are people who did not realize how close they were to success when they gave up."* Even when you think of the many things he invented and the major contributions he made to the way we live our lives, his failures far outnumbered his successes. For every invention he created, there were literally thousands of unsuccessful experiments. By refusing to accept the word "unsuccessful" and viewing these as learning opportunities, he was able to go on until he reached a successful conclusion. He tried, met a temporary defeat, analyzed the reasons for the failure, accepted responsibility and adjusted by trying something new.

This is an extremely important lesson to learn as a salesman. Even if you are the most successful salesman in the history of the world, you will have far more failures than successes. Regardless of your product and regardless of the kind of people to whom you are offering it, you will be rejected far more than you will find acceptance. This is why so many of the things I have written to you are directly related. You must develop confidence and have a solid base from which to work. If you believe in your product or service and what you are doing, you cannot be shaken by someone's refusal to purchase from you on any given presentation. Whether an individual is a stock broker, selling pharmaceuticals, or a manufacturer's representative with a myriad of products, the vast majority of people they see will not become their customers. This does not mean that their product or service has been rejected or that the individual salesman has been rejected. It may mean that the prospect has previous loyalties to others, or that the particular product does not fit their current needs.

In every case of an individual who has achieved greatness, that person has encountered many failures along the road to success. Napoleon said, *"Victory belongs to the most persevering."* Even after a person has achieved what they themselves may consider to be an overall success, they will still encounter day to day failures in reaching their moving goals to accomplish specific objectives.

We are often led to believe that the person who becomes the President of the United States has achieved the pinnacle of success in this country. Let us assume for a moment that this is true. However, each President proceeds to develop his plan for the nation and presents that plan to Congress in the form of various pieces of legislation. No President, not even Franklin Roosevelt, who in many ways revolutionized our society with the introduction of sweeping social change, found success in getting everything he wanted through Congress. I highly recommend that you read Roosevelt's biography. As a young man, he was vibrant and active. He suddenly found himself felled by polio and facing a life on crutches or in a wheelchair. His family had plenty of money and social standing, and he could have resigned himself to a life of being cared for and pitied by those around him. He refused to accept that status in life and rose to become President, to steer the Nation out of the worst depression in its history and to join with Winston Churchill in successfully fighting against Hitler and the evils of the Nazis. I am sure that there were many moments in his life when he wished he could walk and come and go as others did, free of his crutches and his wheelchair. However, wishing he were whole again, and feeling sorry for himself, are two totally different concepts. He never gave up. He persisted by simply refusing to be beaten. He took what life gave him and proceeded to make the most of his life, not only from the standpoint of what he could get out of that life, but also from the standpoint of what he could contribute to others.

In the depths of the depression, Roosevelt inspired his fellow Americans by telling them, *"The only thing we have to fear is fear itself."* Even his most severe political critics, would have to grant him high marks for courage and persistence. If you study his record closely, you will also find many failures in the course of his pursuit of great achievements. Read his life story and refer to it often when events are closing in around you.

My two favorite role models for persistence are Abraham Lincoln and Helen Keller. You've probably seen this list before but it is worth keeping as a reference when you get discouraged. Consider this person's life history:

- He worked in a store which failed in his early 20's
- Had his first love die when she was only 19
- Lost a state legislative race at age 23
- Suffered a nervous collapse at age 27
- Lost an election for Congress at age 34

- After being elected to Congress, was defeated for re-election at age 40
- Had two of his sons die before reaching their teens
- Lost a Senate race in his mid-40's
- Lost a second campaign for the Senate at age 49
- Became President of the United States at age 52

The life history was, of course, that of Abraham Lincoln. What a study in perseverance!

Helen Keller was born deaf and blind. Most people can't even begin to comprehend so catastrophic a condition. And yet, Helen Keller, with the help and commitment of her teacher, Anne Sullivan, overcame her handicaps to become an international celebrity. She was the author of one of my favorite quotations, *"No pessimist ever discovered the secrets of the stars or sailed to an uncharted land or opened a new heaven to the human spirit."* Imagine such beautiful thoughts coming from someone with her handicaps. Think of her plight and her victory whenever you feel down or discouraged.

Read about those who have overcome adversity and develop a file of stories you can refer to when you are feeling troubled or discouraged. Even the most positive thinking individual will have moments of discouragement and even despair. How you deal with those times will determine your ultimate level of success. I never played golf, but I once heard a remark by someone who did play which was applicable to a career in sales. He said, "It isn't the quality of your good shots that determines the kind of player you are, but the quality of your bad shots." In sales, it isn't how you handle the successes you will have as much as how you deal with the inevitable frustrations and failures that will determine your success and especially the longevity of that success. Learning how great people handled their problems, persisted through opposition, and eventually prevailed, will provide you with a set of models you can follow.

2. Build a library of inspirational materials and use them throughout the day, every day. [3] Every salesman will meet with great frustration. You must find a way to deal with this frustration when it arises. The best possible way to deal with these depressing interludes is to prevent them from arising in the first place. I found that by constantly keeping myself motivated and inspired, I would have the strength to ward off the intrusion of negative thoughts.

As you know, from the chapter on organization, I would end each work day by making a "To Do" list for

---

[3] Author's Note: My mother, in later years and after her selling career was over, kept herself constantly inspired by listening to cassette tapes. Tapes, portable tape players, and car players were not available to her during her selling years. Had they been, she would have been a heavy user of the inspirational materials contained on these tapes. The industry of creating and marketing motivational tapes has, of course, become a big business today. She would have been pleased with that development.

the next day. Notice that I said my "work day" ended with the making of a "To Do" list. My actual day ended with the reading of some inspirational material, and each new day began within the first five minutes of my awakening with the reading of other uplifting works. My purpose was to avoid becoming weak to the point that negative thoughts or feelings could crowd out my positive approach.

We are told to keep ourselves strong and hearty to fight off the invasion of disease. And yet, few people use the same approach in keeping their minds free of poisonous thoughts or ideas. You should be at least as diligent in controlling what your mind sees, hears and is exposed to as you are in protecting your physical well-being. It is much easier to prevent a negative idea from ever entering the sanctuary of your mind than to find a way to rid yourself of it once it has taken root.

I normally would not read a lot just before retiring, or just after getting up. It wouldn't take much. A few sentences or a few paragraphs might be enough to keep my aim concentrated on my goals. It wasn't how much I read, but what the words meant to me and how I would react upon seeing or hearing them.

I have already referred to Think and Grow Rich in an earlier letter. That book was a never ending source of inspiration for me. It also served as something of a protective liner in my mind against the intrusion of feelings which would impede my progress toward success. Below is a partial list of other books and materials which I relied on to keep me in a positive mood: <u>The Magic of Believing</u> by Claude M. Bristol, <u>How to Live 365 Days a Year</u> by John A. Schindler, M.D, <u>The Success System that Never Fails</u> by W. Clement Stone, <u>Living a Happy Life</u> by F.A. Magoun, <u>Creative Help for Daily Living</u> by Norman Vincent Peale. The <u>Creative Help for Daily Living</u> publications are small booklets which are reprints of sermons delivered by Dr. Peale. A single excerpt from one of the booklets will give you an idea of the kinds of inspirational materials to be found within the pages of Dr. Peale's publication:

"I know a woman who is a writer, and a very good one. I heard her tell once about her own rebirth as a mother, and as a person, and as a writer. She has an article on what she calls "upbeat words" that if you reverse your thoughts from negative to positive, from evil to good, your life will change.

Let us examine the word evil, meaning everything is bad, everything is unhappy, everything is miserable. The world is evil; the country is evil; people are evil; everything is evil. When you reverse the letters and spell it backwards, you get the word live! Just think of it, you can reverse your life if you reverse your thoughts. Do you think in terms of evil or do you think in terms of live? Things are not so bad; they are going to be good; life is good; the nation will live; I will live! It all depends on what word you are saying."

I am also a great believer in the motivating power

of short quotations. I would use one specific quotation each day. I am setting out for you the actual quotes I used for a one month period:

September 1
"Good people are good because they've come to wisdom through failure."
WILLIAM SAROYAN

September 2
"Education is the ability to listen to almost anything without losing your temper or your self-confidence."
ROBERT FROST

September 3
"To conquer fear is the beginning of wisdom."
BERTRAND RUSSELL

September 4
"Do not be too timid and squeamish about your actions. All life is an experiment."
RALPH WALDO EMERSON

September 5
"You must do the things you think you cannot do."
ELEANOR ROOSEVELT

September 6
'The thing always happens that you really believe in, and the belief in a thing makes it happen."
FRANK LLOYD WRIGHT

September 7
"Lack of something to feel important about is almost the greatest tragedy a man can have."
DR. ARTHUR F. MORGAN

September 8
"What others think you are isn't as important as what you know yourself to be."
MY SALES MANAGER

September 9
"The essence of courage is not that your heart should not quake but that nobody else should know that it does."
E.F. BENSON

September 10
"He had occasional flashes of silence that made his conversation perfectly delightful."
SYDNEY SMITH

September 11
"I desire so to conduct the affairs of this Administration that if at the end, when I come to lay down the reins of power, I have lost every other friend on earth, I shall at least have one friend left and that friend shall be down inside me."
ABRAHAM LINCOLN

September 12
"We judge ourselves by what we feel
capable of doing while others judge us
by what we have already done."
HENRY WADSWORTH LONGFELLOW

September 13
"Speak less than thou knoweth."
WILLIAM SHAKESPEARE

September 14
"To know oneself, one should assert oneself.
Psychology is action, not thinking about oneself."
ALBERT CAMUS

September 15
"Whatever the mind of man can conceive
and believe, it can achieve."
NAPOLEON HILL

September 16
"Imagination is more important than knowledge."
ALBERT EINSTEIN

September 17
"A life spent in making mistakes is not only
more honorable, but more useful than a
life spent in doing nothing."
GEORGE BERNARD SHAW

September 18
"You can't build a reputation on what
you're going to do."
HENRY FORD

September 19
"Cast out all negative thoughts and fill the
mind with positive thoughts."
NORMAN VINCENT PEALE

September 20
1 am going to keep my attitude and thinking
calm and cheerful — RIGHT NOW!"
JOHN A. SCHINDLER, M.D.

September 21
"Back your belief with a resolute will
and you become unconquerable."
CLAUDE M. BRISTOL

September 22
Do it now!"
W. CLEMENT STONE

September 23
Know what you wish to say,
say it with all the emotional feeling
at your command, then sit down."
NAPOLEON HILL

September 24
"Day by day in every way,
I am getting better and better."
DR. EMILE COVE

September 25
"You become what you think."
W. CLEMENT STONE

September 26
"Success is achieved by those who try."
W. CLEMENT STONE

September 27
"To reach the part of Heaven we must sail sometimes
with the wind and sometimes against it. But we must
sail, and not drift nor lie at anchor."
OLIVER WENDELL HOLMES

September 28
"Man is what he believes."
ANTON CHEKHOV

September 29
"Every man's memory is his private literature."
ALDOUS HUXLEY

September 30
"The mind is its own place and in itself can make a
heaven of Hell, a hell of Heaven."
JOHN MILTON

I would never begin a day without a quote to inspire and motivate me. Upon arising I would write the quote out on an index card in longhand. This would force me to think about the words as I wrote them. Then throughout the day I would pull out the index card and read the words out loud to myself. I didn't just mouth the words in an empty, meaningless recitation. I tried to emotionalize the words and make my quotations a significant guidepost for that particular day. It is hard to get discouraged or depressed when you constantly fill your mind with inspirational words.

I could go on and on listing the specific books and articles I have used to motivate myself. However, new books and articles will be written. New messages will be developed and more inspiring ways of delivery will be created by tomorrow's messengers. Open yourself to receive this kind of information. Develop your own list of materials which you rely on to maintain the right kind of attitude.

Let me leave you with one important reminder before going to the next topic. Be ever vigilant in protecting your mind from negative intruders! You brush your teeth and comb your hair every day. You don't perform those jobs one day and then skip a few days. You must be just as diligent in practicing mind protection and preservation as you are in maintaining your body. If you do, you will find it much easier to maintain the positive frame of mind which is an essential characteristic of the successful salesperson.

3. Recall successful past experiences. Record, remember, and dwell on your accomplishments. Accept a defeat as a learning experience and forget it. Replay over and over in your mind, those things which have been successful for you. Grow to anticipate success.

As I indicated earlier, confidence must precede success. However, once some success has been achieved, that success can become a building block in maintaining confidence. The more success, the more confidence, and the more confidence, the more success one has. That is why I strongly urge you to dwell on your accomplishments. It is not enough to simply record and remember these events, but you must immerse yourself in them.

Let me give you an example from my own experience. After I had been with the company for a few years, I was asked by my sales manager to make a presentation to the periodic sales meetings of all the representatives within our district. I described these meetings to you in my first letter. At the time, I was quite new to public speaking and was extremely nervous about making the presentation. However, I was determined to make my sales manager proud of me and to establish myself, not only in his eyes, but in the eyes of my peers, as someone who could handle this kind of presentation.

I practiced my presentation and was confident that the subject matter I had been asked to discuss was something about which I was well equipped to lead the group.

My sales manager gave me an excellent introduction, saying several nice things abut my recent efforts. With that he turned over the stage to me. I remember walking up and being consumed by a feeling of total confidence and power. I knew that I could make the presentation and thoroughly cover all points I had been asked to examine. As I moved into the body of my presentation, I began to feel even more comfortable and more confident, not only in my product knowledge, but in the way people were responding to what I had to say. At the end of my presentation there were a number of questions. Each question I handled easily, and at the conclusion of the final question, what began as polite applause, ended in a standing ovation. I have never felt more confident in my life. That feeling is etched into my memory forever. I had been confident because I was prepared, and because of the combination of preparation and confidence, I performed well.

As a result of that performance, I had an experience to draw upon. Whenever I had a tough meeting scheduled or a difficult problem to deal with, I started by recalling how I felt on that exciting occasion. Normally, I would sit quietly and take several deep breaths to put myself in a state of complete relaxation. At that point I relive, in every possible detail, what occurred during my presentation to my peer group. I don't just recall being there and having it go well, but I recall vividly in my mind what I was wearing, every word my sales manager said in introducing me and the feeling of power and confidence and control that I felt as I walked to the podium. I recall the first few words that I spoke and the fact that I was able to speak with total confidence without ever referring to a note. I recall each question asked of me by a member of the audience. I remember what each person who asked a question was wearing and the inflections in their voices when a question was asked. I see myself standing there and hear the words I spoke to the audience, the questions they were directing to me, and the responses I gave them.

I thus involved my visual sense in watching myself and the members of the audience. I involved my sense of hearing by listening to every detail from the introduction, to the presentation, to the specific questions which were asked, and my responses to those questions. I had goose bumps crawling up and down my body as the applause rang out from members of the audience. I remember how I felt walking off the stage, not just that I felt good, but the physical sensation of having a warm glow which seemed to envelope my entire body. Each of these senses is important in recalling the event.

It is important that in recalling a past event, the recollection involves all the senses. This opens multiple channels into your brain and makes it easier for you to repeat the feelings generated by that positive experience.

You must develop the feeling to the very core of your being of what that success feels like. You then must find a way to conjure up that feeling at times when you want to repeat the past success. This too is an art which can be practiced. Remember how you felt at a particular time when you felt extremely confident. Then, when you need that feeling to deal with a current situation, recall in the most vivid terms possible the feeling that you had when you achieved that past success. This is a vital lesson for you to learn. You must always remember how you felt at the time when great success was achieved and you must remember how to duplicate that feeling within yourself. Never believe anyone who tells you that this is impossible.

While I want you to know it is not impossible, I do not tell you that it is easy. It must be practiced over and over again. Practice sitting in a dark room. Close your eyes and visualize in whatever way possible, what you saw and what you felt, and the inner most thoughts you had at the time you achieved a particularly great success. Practice the ability to recreate this feeling over and over until you can pull it up easily.

Through practice and experience, I discovered another significant truth about reliving successful events. I didn't have to actually live them, I could make them up! Early in my career there were very few successful past experiences for me to draw upon. However, I was blessed with a feeling of destiny that I would find the success I was seeking. Therefore, it was easy for me to make up events and have them all result in happy endings. I found that from the standpoint of inspiration, my mind reacted the same way to a vividly imagined event as it did to an event which actually occurred. This opened a whole new world of exciting experiences.

One of the most liberating realizations in the world is that human beings are able to change the past in two ways. You can replay earlier events which did not work out as you had hoped. In these replays you can change the facts and turn bad to good or sad to happy. You can literally change in your mind whatever occurred into what you would like to have occurred.

The second way you can change the past is to leave the events as they were but alter your reaction to those events. Dale Carnegie said, "It is the way we react to circumstances that determines our feelings." Once you realize that you, and only you can control your own thoughts you are able to rewrite events or your reaction to those events to create a whole new past from which you can draw memories.

The great thing about making up events was that I was limited only by my own imagination. I could put the most difficult prospect in my imaginary scene and have them say yes over and over again. I would rehearse difficult assignments until they didn't seem so difficult. Whenever failure and rejection would pile up, I would dismiss those events from my memory and replace them with imaginary events which were successful. Details were the key to using imaginary events as a defense to rejection. I wouldn't just imagine that I met with a prospect and they bought my product. I went through every possible detail in my mind. I was aware of the clothes I was wearing and what my prospect was wearing. I saw the furniture in the room and was aware of the carpet, the wallpaper, and what was hanging on the walls.

I would hear my presentation and see the facial gestures by my prospect. I would hear the prospect's questions and comments as well as my responses. I would play the scene out so literally that we would occasionally be interrupted by a phone call or a receptionist, but the interruption would not hamper my march toward a successful conclusion. In my imaginary sales presentations, the customer always said yes!

You now have a three step program which if practiced, I assure will give you the strength to persevere:

1. **Read the biographies of great people.**

2. **Build a library of inspirational materials and use them throughout the day, every day.**

3. **Recall successful past experiences.**

Follow these steps and persevere. Never give up. Try. Taste defeat. Accept that defeat as a temporary

Chapter Ten

STRIVE TO BE DIFFERENT

*"That so few dare to be eccentric,
marks the chief danger of our time."*
— JOHN STUART MILL

Dear Son,

Now the fun begins. Strive to be different. Hopefully, you will find learning the lessons of breathing properly, goal setting, working on yourself, organization, and the rest of my advice to be challenging, rewarding, and fulfilling. However, following my advice in all of these areas will require commitment and hard work. The fun will come in the results you achieve. If you follow my advice and strive to be different, however, you can have fun during the process.

Don't be afraid to be embarrassed. Use your creativity. Stretch your imagination with no boundary or limits. Seek advice from others who have been successful. You will find in most cases that they have been successful because in some shape, form, or fashion, they have broken barriers and been different. The great actress, Tallulah Bankhead, once said, *"Nobody can be exactly like me. Sometimes even I have trouble doing it."* She was truly one of a kind. That was why she not only had initial success in her career, but had great longevity. She could not be replaced. She was too unique!

In my case, it was easy to be different in at least one respect. I was a woman. As the first saleswoman in my field, clients were either curious, defensive, or overly courteous. They always reacted differently than they would had I been what they were used to dealing with — a man. I constantly tried to be different in other ways. Being different involved taking risks.

Since this chapter is about being different, I decided to take a different tactic in demonstrating the benefits I gained from taking the unusual approach rather than following conventional methods. I did many things to be different. I was not afraid of risks, and I was not intimidated by the prospect of failure. I knew setbacks would only be temporary and that conviction would free me to be creative. I am going to tell you a story about one situation in which I took a risk and was willing to be different.

First, let me give you a bit of background. I smile to myself when recalling some of the initial reactions from clients whom I was calling on for the first time. When I would schedule an appointment, I would appear on the client's book as Lee Ledbetter. I gather that they always assumed a man would be calling on them. When I appeared, the reactions were strange and varied.

The worst initial reaction I ever received evolved into one of my best client relationships. After scheduling the meeting by phone, I arrived on time to meet with an especially busy doctor who was engaged in a general practice and whose patients were mostly wealthy and socially prominent individuals. His receptionist had been with him for over twenty years and was fiercely protective of his time and his personal habits. As always, I looked around the office upon my arrival, seeking information about my prospect. What I saw wasn't encouraging. His office was not well kept. The magazines were mostly about hunting and fishing. He had a variety of stuffed animal trophies affixed to the walls. They seemed to glare down at me as if to suggest that they fully expected to see my head alongside theirs in the near future. I had never been hunting in my life and grew angry when I saw animals being mistreated. I had no understanding or patience for animals being killed for sport by hunters.

I had also done my usual research on the prospect before appearing for my initial visit. I had not found much good news there either. He was a hunter who took great pleasure in blasting away at small animals or big game in Africa. He was a person who harbored racial and religious prejudices and, as you know, I have always been tolerant of others regardless of their race, religion or background. I take great pride as a parent knowing that you learned the lesson of tolerance well and have made it a cornerstone of your life.

My research found other interesting things about my prospect. He went to a state school in the deep south and was a fiercely loyal alumnus; I had not even attended college. He belonged to the oldest country club in town. Membership was based more on one's family tree than on achievement. I would not have been asked to join if I had suddenly inherited millions of dollars. He smoked cigars, a habit which I found disgusting. My immediate predecessor, who had represented the company before I took over the district, had met with this doctor only once and could never again schedule an appointment. In briefing me as I took over, my predecessor suggested that I not even waste my time calling on this "hard-nosed old coot".

There was more bad news. He belonged to one political party and I had regularly voted for the other. He liked horses; I had never ridden one. He liked to spend time fishing; I couldn't even swim and hated being in the water. He wasn't close to his children and spent very little time with his grandchildren.

Why did I bother? Well, there were several reasons. The company wanted me to pursue business with this doctor. They knew his reputation and knew what it would mean in terms of public relations if we could find a way to do business with him. It was also a personal challenge for me. I felt like Dr. Mills (not his real name) today, tomorrow, the world. I knew that doing business with him would give me confidence to attack other difficult situations. I also knew that there was no downside. If I failed, everyone would say it was to be expected and would find no fault in my effort. If I succeeded, it would put me on the map in the eyes of my company and my industry. It would also be a great confidence boost and a success on which I could build.

My research was not all pessimistic. It had also given me some slight encouragement. I learned that my prospect had been a decorated war hero. He was a legend for his bravery among those who had served with him. I felt this might give me an opening. I also found that his wife, while lovingly devoted to him, was quite different from him in several key aspects. She was active in a number of charitable causes and was tolerant of people of different races and religions. She was described by several people as a "really caring person". She loved her two children deeply and doted on her four grandchildren. She had also had an encounter with cancer and had survived extensive surgery and follow up treatments. Thus, we had much in common. I felt that his proven courage and her background provided a possible avenue for me to follow in creating a business relationship with this admittedly challenging individual.

Let me pick up the story as I sat in his office. I assumed before scheduling my first meeting that it would be difficult, and in the best of all worlds, would require a series of meetings and a lot of time and effort. I promised his receptionist that I only needed five minutes and that is all I was given. I had already stepped outside and used my breathing technique. I was well versed on my product and was fully prepared to answer any questions he might ask. I was using my best posture and felt confident. When the receptionist called my name, I strode purposefully down the hallway into his private office. He sat behind a huge desk in a large overstuffed chair with a cigar in his mouth and appeared to be a giant caricature of a doctor. I extended my hand and said, "Hello, Doctor Mills, I'm Lee Ledbetter." He took my hand in his huge palm, shook it nonchalantly, and in a most condescending manner said, "Hello, girlie."

In that instant, I made the decision that this meeting would not be productive no matter what I did or said. I felt that to push him in any way would have closed the door on my ever being able to see him again. I decided it would be best to briefly introduce myself and hope to return to this particular field when the playing conditions were better. I remained standing since he didn't offer me a seat. I looked him in the eye and said, "You were kind enough to give me five minutes, and I will repay your kindness by not using all that time." I laid a few brief pieces of literature on his desk and said, "Here is some information on my company and several of our products. I will be in touch through the mail with items of interest to you, and hopefully, you will see fit to give me more time at some point in the future. Thank you very much." I spun on my heel and walked out. Elapsed time ... 30 seconds. He had a shocked look on his face and I knew I had accomplished my goal of being different. Now it was time to begin phase two.

Phase two was a risk but one which I felt was worth taking. I got the home address and telephone number of Dr. Mills and called his home. I asked to speak to his wife. The lady who answered the phone asked my name which I gave to her. Within a few seconds, Mrs. Mills picked up the phone and said in a very friendly manner, "Yes, this is Mrs. Mills. What can I do for you?"

I said, "This is Lee Ledbetter. I would like to have an opportunity to spend a few minutes with you in your home."

To my great shock, without any questions or hesitation, her response was, "Certainly, when would you like to come by?"

I said, "How about tomorrow morning at 9 o'clock." I had a cancellation the next day and did have an opening and thought I should try for the earliest possible opportunity to meet with her. She said that would be fine, and to my great surprise, said she looked forward to meeting with me.

Upon hanging up the phone, I sat and thought for several moments, but was unable to clear up my confusion. Why had she been so friendly? Why had she agreed to meet with me? Why had she not asked any questions as to who I was and why I wanted to meet with her? Why did she not inquire as to what my request was all about? Maybe, most mysteriously, why did she not suggest that I was quite rude to be calling her and asking for a meeting with no explanation? It was useless to try and answer any of these questions. Answers would have to wait until the next morning.

I drove up to the front of her beautiful home the next day at five minutes to nine. I stepped out of the car and strode purposefully towards her door. I did not have my briefcase or any material about my company because that was not the purpose of this visit. As I stood at the doorway, I took several deep breaths and decided that I really had nothing to lose and would treat this as an interesting adventure no matter what might happen. With that, I rang the bell and waited. I expected a housekeeper or maid to answer the door, but within a few moments, Mrs. Mills herself opened the door and extended her hand to me.

"Hello, my name is Carolyn. Welcome to my home.

Won't you come in please."

I was taken aback by her friendly nature and became even more confused as to why she was being so nice. We walked through the foyer to the living room. She offered me a seat and then asked if I would like to join her in a cup of coffee. I said yes. She left and in a few minutes, returned with a silver tray and china cups full of coffee. Cream and sugar were on the tray. She put cream but no sugar in her coffee. I told her I would drink mine black.

At that point, she sat down across from me in a large, heavily cushioned chair. I was on the couch and had taken in the beautiful furnishings of the room around me. I complimented her on what a beautiful home she had. She thanked me very much for the comment and after taking two sips of her coffee, leaned forward and placed her cup and saucer on the coffee table. Just as I was about to speak, she spoke first.

"You cannot imagine how surprised I was when you called and asked to see me. I don't know you personally but feel like I know you very well. Let me explain."

"Several years ago, I was diagnosed with breast cancer and had a radical mastectomy. I will never forget the despair I felt at the time of my initial diagnosis and the even greater despair I felt lying in the hospital bed feeling sorry for myself. I was sure that even if I survived I would never be a complete human being again.

The first day I was able to receive visitors, a young lady knocked softly on my door and asked if she could visit with me. I nodded slowly and invited her in. She pulled up a chair, sat next to me, reached out and took my hand in hers and suggested that we say a short prayer together. We did that without my knowing who she was or why she was there. But, I do recall that the words of her prayer seemed to be so personal and full of understanding for the situation I was in. After the prayer, she told me that she had undergone similar surgery almost four years earlier. She spent almost an hour with me, telling me everything she had gone through and preparing me for what I would have to do next. Our conversation proceeded from the very general to the very specific. She advised me on how to deal with everything from the physical pain to the psychological trauma. We talked about how she and others who had been in this position had dealt with their husbands."

"From the moment she left my room, I stopped feeling sorry for myself and began to view this as just another challenge in life. She has remained a close friend and confidant from that day forward. As a matter of fact, I called her excitedly last night to let her know that you were coming by to see me today. You see, the thing I haven't told you thus far is that she told me that following her surgery, you walked into her room and did the same thing for her that she had done for me. She spoke glowingly of your heart, your courage, your caring for others, and how you were always there for women like herself. Even though we never met, I

felt like I knew you extremely well. You were her heroine and according to her, the heroine of many other
women in this city. I had written letters to her and
exchanged calls and, as I indicated, we have become
close friends."

"I am embarrassed and apologetic to you for the fact
that I have never taken the time to express my thanks
to you. It was like a message from heaven when you
called yesterday. I really had no idea why you wanted
to see me, but I knew it would be an opportunity to
thank you from the bottom of my heart for all the
things you had done for me."

At this point, she began to cry softly and I got up
from the couch and moved toward her. She rose and we
embraced in the middle of her living room each sobbing
on the other's shoulders. I will never forget the moment
and how close I felt to this woman with whom, despite
the great differences in our lives, I had so much in common. On the surface, we appeared to have nothing in
common. She was married to a wealthy doctor; I was a
divorced mother of a young son. She spent time in
social and charitable activities and had never worked
for a paycheck in her life. I was struggling to make
ends meet, and the process of making a living, at that
stage, was my first priority. And yet, illness cut across
all those differences and gave us a large plot of common
ground on which to stand.

After we sat back down, we talked for almost two hours about other women we had known and how they had handled their experiences. The conversation became highly personal in terms of caring for ourselves and how we were able to adjust to living with ourselves in the altered condition resulting from the surgery.

At one point, I almost forgot my original intent for going to see her. I knew that I had made a friend for life, and that I would enjoy this friendship regardless of whether any positive business results were ever forthcoming. However, some two hours after arriving, I did say to her, "You are probably wondering why I asked to see you. I also should apologize for my aggressive behavior, but I felt I had nothing to lose. It was almost like I was drawn to call on you and after what has occurred this morning, there may very well be something to that feeling."

"After the serious nature of the things we have talked about, I almost feel guilty about telling you the real reason for my visit. However, feeling guilty is something that has never troubled me in my life so let me be honest with you."

"I recently became a pharmaceutical sales representative for a major drug company. Your husband is one of the doctors I have been assigned to call on. You are well aware, I am sure, that your husband is very busy, very hard to schedule an appointment with, and a difficult person to do business with."

She smiled knowingly and said, "Yes, I am well aware of all of those things. I would expect that as a woman, you will have even greater difficulty than most in getting him to write prescriptions for your products."

I smiled and replied, "I could not have said it better myself."

She then sat back in her chair and looked me in the eye and said, "You mean to tell me that you had the nerve to come here and explain to me your situation in hopes that I would help you do business with my husband?"

I looked back and began to wonder if the two hour friendship was about to come to an early end. At that point, I had no choice but to proceed full speed ahead.

"Well, to be honest with you, that is exactly right. I have always believed that you never know until you ask, and I knew that if I pursued conventional methods of doing business with your husband that it would never work. I just decided to come talk to you, woman to woman, and see if there would be some way that you could help me, not only in dealing with your husband, but as a doctor's wife, to see what advice you could give me to best succeed in this career. I am raising a young son, and I am committed to doing whatever it takes to be successful. For that reason, I don't apologize for being here and hope you will understand why I was so aggressive."

At that point, she gave one of the kindest laughs I have ever heard in my life and said, "Everything I have ever heard about you is certainly true. You are a miracle lady." From that point on, she and I were fast friends. To this day, she still calls me the "miracle lady".

She went on to say, "First let me compliment you on having the courage to do what you have done. I very easily could have refused your request for an appointment, or thrown you out of the house when you appeared."

"Yes," I interrupted, "but if that had happened I would have been no worse for having tried the experiment."

"Well, I suppose you are right. But now, let's get down to it. How can I help you do business with my husband?" she asked herself out loud. She then made several specific suggestions, but within the next few months, she went far beyond these initial suggestions. She set up meetings for me. She asked me to accompany her and her husband to numerous social events. Her husband became more than a good client. He became my primary source for referral business. He constantly made suggestions as to how I could improve my approach and my presentations. But most importantly, he became a true friend. Proudly, through the joint efforts of his wife and me, we were able to alter some of his beliefs and help make changes in his lifestyle. In his later years, he became more tolerant of others, gave up hunting for gardening, and he even stopped smoking those horrible cigars!

In hindsight, my decision to approach her directly and ask to visit with her was the turning point in my career. I took a risk. I did something totally different, totally outside the normal range of expected behavior for someone in my field, and it worked! I have taken a long time telling you this story but I think it is essential for you to understand the importance of finding new and unusual ways of approaching prospective clients. Don't study the habits of mediocre performers. Study the practices of high achievers. You will find that those successful individuals dared to be different. Given my own experiences, I began to keenly observe those who were highly successful in their particular fields. The one common thread which the peak performers had in common was that they were unique. They had run the risk of facing ridicule from their peers and competitors because they stood apart from the pack. They weren't like everyone else and that very uniqueness was the key to their success.

I investigated the personal histories of as many of these unique individuals as possible. Kemmons Wilson realized that interstate highways would change America's driving habits. He knew that thousands of new rooms would be needed to accommodate the new breed of travelers. At a time when most people were used to staying in tourist cabins, he created Holiday Inn and changed the expectations of highway travelers.

John Shea, a Memphis ear surgeon, had the courage to withstand the criticism of many of his peers. As a result, his revolutionary procedure has restored sound to the lives of thousands of people around the world.

Elvis Presley refused to accept the advice of "experts" that he change both his music and his stage mannerisms. He insisted on retaining his individuality and refused to become something he wasn't. As a result, he became the *King of Rock'n Roll*.

Clarence Saunders believed, contrary to all the advice he was given, that shoppers would prefer to buy all their groceries in one store rather than traipse to the baker, the butcher, and the vegetable stand. His vision led to the modern day supermarket. Creation of these "magnet" stores attracted shoppers in large numbers and resulted in the development of shopping centers.

I have chosen the four individuals named above to illustrate my point for a particular reason. They all were from my hometown. I knew them all personally and even though I didn't know Elvis as well as the others, I met him on several occasions, had him in our home, and was well acquainted with many people who were close to him. Because these four individuals were local, it was easy for me to study their habits and their success. I was able to ask direct questions and learn first hand how committed they were to their personal set of principles. They were all courageous. They were all pioneers. They will each have a legacy unmatched by multitudes of their peers who sought only acceptance, and in doing so, found failure or mediocrity.

Chart your own course. No matter what your product or service may be, you will have many competitors with the same or similar offerings. Your ability to market yourself will be more important in determining your ultimate level of success than the marketing of your product. Buyers want to have fun. Many of them are bored with their lives and their careers. Strive to be a fresh breeze which blows through their lives on a regular basis. Many of my clients have told me that they looked forward to my visits because they never knew what to expect. What a compliment! They were literally curious as to what outrageous, interesting, bizarre, and unusual thing I would do next. Be a source of entertainment for your clients. You won't succeed with everyone. You may even offend someone occasionally. Don't be dissuaded by negative reactions. Commit to a course of being unique. You will not only be more successful, you will also get a lot more out of the ride.

All my love,
Mother

Chapter Eleven

TAKE ACTION

*"He who waits to do a great deal of good
at once, will never do anything."*
— SAMUEL JOHNSON

Dear Son,

The most important word in the English language is love. I hope that my earlier letters have demonstrated how important love is in our everyday lives and in building a successful career. As vital a role as love plays in any successful life, my experience has taught me that without applying the second most important word in the English language, very little can be accomplished. That word is ACTION!

~ from Mother, with Love ~

Hopefully, my letters will help motivate you to achieve great things. But, remember, the purpose of reading motivational material is to create action. Don't think about doing something and then fail to do it. Thought without action adds up to nothing.

Do it! Act! Make something happen!

Most people squander their talents. I am less amazed at how some people do so much, than I am over why most people do so little. Henry Wadsworth Longfellow wrote, *"The talent of success is nothing more than doing what you can do well and doing well whatever you do."* My sales manager had a saying which he repeated often to me, *"A vision without a task is but a dream. A task without a vision becomes drudgery."* He believed that talk could get you an opportunity but that only action could turn the opportunity into an accomplishment.

Don't let your most creative thoughts die. Put them into action and change them from an idea to an accomplishment. Many people I have known have talked a great game but failed to follow up. Andrew Carnegie said, *"As I grow older, I pay less attention to what men say. I just watch what they do."* Benjamin Franklin agreed when he said, *"Well done is better than well said."*

I have a dear friend who is a physical therapist. She has spent many years caring for aging and ill patients in several local nursing homes. She once told me a story which had a profound influence on the way I have tried to live my life. She said that of the many elderly patients she had worked with, not a single one had expressed any regret over what they had done in life. However, the vast majority of her patients shared strong regret over those things which they had not done.

Make your life a life of action. Do everything possible to avoid looking back on your life with regret and disappointment over what you failed to do. It is alright to make mistakes. Expect to make mistakes. Learn from them and push on. One of the principles of my career was to make errors of commission rather than errors of omission. Those persons who build their career around avoiding errors of commission may make good bureaucrats or doorkeepers but they will never reach a position of leadership or achieve lasting success. That kind of accomplishment is left to those who accept challenges and are willing to accept the criticisms which come from their willingness to make errors of commission. Emma Goldman, a Russian born American lecturer and editor wrote, *"Idealists ... foolish enough to throw caution to the wind ... have advanced mankind and have enriched the world."*

What if Columbus had been unwilling to make errors of commission? Or Edison? Or Jonas Salk? Or Franklin Roosevelt? Or Churchill? The list can go on and on. Now make a list of famous bureaucrats or functionaries who based their lives and careers on making only errors of omission. Can't think of any? That's funny, neither can I. Which list would you rather be on? The answer is obvious. Take flight. Soar. Be brave. Be daring. Accept the risk that goes with making errors of commission and strive for greatness. Don't accept defeat and mediocrity before you ever begin. Build your career based on being willing to make errors of commission rather than errors of omission.

Decide those things you most want. Define them carefully so you can see, hear, feel, taste, and smell those things. Set aside other things which are less important to you. Don't be distracted by things which would not advance you toward your goals. And then act. Do whatever is required to have or get what is truly important to you.

If you wait for all the conditions to be perfect before deciding to act, you will probably accomplish nothing. Seldom do all the stars fall into perfect alignment. W.R. Sweatt was the founder of Minneapolis Honeywell. Under his picture in the boardroom was written one of my favorite quotations:

> *"I will always strive for perfection and will never be satisfied with anything less. But, if I must choose between action today and perfection tomorrow, I will always choose action."*

Use these words to direct your career. Act. W.R. Sweatt was willing to make errors of commission and that willingness allowed him to build a great company. Horace Mann also preferred action. He wrote, *"I have never heard anything about the resolutions of the Disciples but a great deal about the acts of the Apostles."*

Most salespeople work on commission. They are, for all practical purposes, independent contractors. I never felt that I earned a percentage of what I sold. In my mind I paid out a percentage of what I sold to get a variety of support services. The company, in return for a percentage of my sales, provided products, promotional material, secretarial help, and a myriad of other services. I considered myself self-employed with a contractual relationship which provided me with all the necessary back-up. To give anything less than my best effort would be dishonest to my provider of support. But I also owed that same level of performance to myself. Commission sales demands action. If you don't take action, you don't sell and if you don't sell, you don't eat. That is another reason I enjoyed being in sales. Many salaried individuals I know seemed to find a comfort zone. They knew they were going to get paid as long as they did enough to keep their jobs. Many of them became content and made only errors of omission rather than commission.

Don't ever become comfortable and use that status as an excuse for becoming passive and forsaking action. Go to the next level. Seek out new challenges and create new opportunities. Don't ever stop growing.

My mother loved me. I have no doubt of that. But, she came from a poor, rural background and had little understanding for risk or adventure. She believed in playing it safe. She experienced the worst of the Great Depression, and it left an indelible impression on her psyche. She always urged me to play it safe. "If you step out there and it doesn't work, you could wind up with a broken heart," she would say.

Sometimes we are inspired by what other people do. At other times we are inspired by what people fail to do because we vow not to follow in their footsteps. Although I was well into adulthood before finding the necessary courage, I was determined that risk and adventure would be my friends and allies and not strangers. I was determined that you would not have to wait so long to understand the importance of knowing the joy and exhilaration one derives from taking courageous stands and moving forward.

A minister for whom I always had great respect and affection once told me that a parent should give children "legs to run on and a nest to return to." I wanted you to feel comfortable in testing your legs but to know that you had the comfort of a waiting nest. One of the differences between childhood and being grown up is that the nest may well not be there for the grown-up. You must therefore build your own nest which is the security which comes from knowing yourself and realizing that you are not what you do. Be willing to test your legs knowing that a fall is only an inconvenience, not a threat to your inner self. Treat every situation as an opportunity to learn, not a demand that you prove yourself. Taking that approach will give you the freedom to act.

In order to move forward, you must keep your eyes focused on what lies in front of you. Resentment destroys progress. You can't move forward if you are looking behind you. Don't harbor resentment against anyone whom you feel impeded your progress in the past. Such feelings are counterproductive. Forgive those who have been your enemies or who have served as obstacles to your progress. Turn the page and go forward. Look ahead; don't look backward.

Also, don't let past mistakes keep you from taking action. Many people fail to act because they feel they have made mistakes earlier in life and feel they cannot overcome the results of those actions. I reject that notion. I believe strongly in the words of the English writer, George Eliot, who wrote, *"It is never too late to be what you might have been."*

One of the most successful people I have ever known was, when I first met him and still is, a recovering alcoholic. His life story is an inspiring study in overcoming past mistakes.

He had married his high school sweetheart and they both worked while he got his college degree. She worked full-time and he worked part-time. They had two children while he was in school. After his graduation he took a sales position with a prestigious national firm.

In college he had started drinking on a regular basis. He would have a few drinks before dinner, then "nurse a few" during the evening and then have a nightcap before going to bed. He never really considered himself a drinker, just someone who "had a few drinks." He was an immediate success in his job. With a loving wife, two wonderful children and a great job, he appeared to have an unlimited future. But within a few years he had lost it all. He became a hopeless, helpless alcoholic driven only by a desire for his next drink. He lost his promising job. He then went through several other jobs but was fired from those as well.

His wife left him and moved to another state where her parents had retired. She took the children with her. Within a few years, she remarried and he lost all contact with his children. He was arrested several times and was hospitalized on two separate occasions. He was about as far down as an individual could get. But then a wonderful thing happened to him. A friend from his high school days had dealt with a severe drinking problem of his own and was in recovery after becoming involved in Alcoholics Anonymous.

My friend had tried to stop drinking and go straight on his own but had never been able to succeed. Through the influence and support of his former classmate he finally took the action he needed to take. He became active in AA and told me recently that he had not had a drink in over twenty years.

He was able to persuade a business associate of his father's that he was someone worth taking a chance on. He was hired in a sales position on a probationary status. He had wasted five years of his life, squandered his talents, and had lost his family. It would have been easy for him to decide that life was over for him and that it would be useless to try to start again. But he refused to accept the damage he had done to himself as a permanent barrier. He prospered quickly in his new job and was promoted steadily. Upon the retirement of the company founder, he purchased the company and took it to new heights. He remarried, had two children, and reconciled with the children from his first marriage. What a remarkable comeback!

Past mistakes left scars but he refused to allow those mistakes to destroy the years he had left. With a strong support system to rely on he took action, regained his shattered self-esteem and became a success in the business.

In addition to his business success he has devoted countless hours to charitable causes and has worked tirelessly to help other recovering alcoholics. He told me recently that of the many recovering alcoholics he had hired to work in his company only one had fallen back into a life of drinking and failure. He not only had taken action to salvage his own life, but having saved himself, he set about saving as many others as possible. He was living proof that it is possible to become what we set out to be no matter what we may have been.

You should take the action necessary to constantly improve yourself and to be a success in your career. You should also take action to become a positive force in your community and in the lives of those around you.

The following poem was written on a sheet of paper and handed to me one Sunday morning by a member of my church congregation. The poem was accompanied by a note which I took as a great compliment. The note read, "This poem puts into words what I see you putting into action every day."

Wouldn't this world be a different place
if we began each day
with the thought of helping someone
that we meet along the way?
If we set out with a little prayer
that through the day we'd find
a chance to leave some sunshine
and some happiness behind?

Put the poem on a card and carry it in your briefcase. Read it often. Let it be a reminder to never forget those less fortunate than yourself. Use it as a positive reminder to spread joy and do good work.

Don't wait until tomorrow to express your feelings to your loved ones, your clients, or your acquaintances. Dwight Eisenhower wrote following the death of his father, *"My only regret is that it was always so difficult to let him know the great depth of my affection for him."* Overcome the difficulty in expressing your feelings by doing it often enough that such expressions come easily to you. Don't hold feelings inside until it is too late. Take action and express your inner feelings.

I doubt that I have given you any original ideas in all the letters I have written. My purpose was not to impress you with my originality or to even inspire you to think. My purpose was to motivate you into action. Dale Carnegie wrote, *"The ideas I stand for are not mine. I borrowed them from Socrates. I swiped them from Chesterfield. I stole them from Jesus. And, I put them in a book. If you don't like their rules, whose would you use?"*

Thomas Huxley wrote, *"The great end of life is not knowledge but action."*

Take one idea or thought I have given you and put it into action. That would be better than contemplating everything I've suggested until you have mastered the words and can recite their meaning but have taken not a single action.

~ from Mother, with Love ~

These letters have been a labor of love for me. Read them. Study them. Use them in the spirit of love with which they were written. Share them with others if you choose. But most importantly, use them to inspire yourself to take action.

All my love,
Mother